His Hands on Earth

Courage, Compassion, Charism
and the
Missionary Sisters
of the Sacred Heart of Jesus

Other Books in New London Librarium's
Catholic Series

To the Ends of the Earth:
Memoir of a Missionary Sister of the Sacred Heart of Jesus

Love and Death in the Kingdom of Swaziland

Amore e Morte nel Regno dello Swaziland

Promised Land:
A Nun's Struggle against Landlessness, Lawlessness, Slavery,
Poverty, Corruption, Injustice,
and Environmental Devastation in Amazonia

Be Revolutionary: Some Thoughts from Pope Francis

for Mother Frances Xavier Cabrini

His Hands on Earth: Courage, Compassion, Charism, and the Missionary Sisters of the Sacred Heart of Jesus
by Glenn Alan Cheney

Cover Art, *Never Forgotten (detail)*, by Colleen Hennessy

Copyright © 2017 Glenn Alan Cheney

Published by
New London Librarium
P.O. Box 284
Hanover, CT 06350 — USA
NLLibrarium.com

All rights reserved. No part of this book may be reproduced without express permission from the publisher.

ISBNs
Hardcover: 978-1-947074-03-3
Paperback: 978-1-947074-01-9
eBook: 978-1-947074-02-6
Large Print: 978-1-947074-06-4

PRINTED IN THE UNITED STATES

His Hands on Earth

Courage, Compassion, Charism and the Missionary Sisters of the Sacred Heart of Jesus

Glenn Alan Cheney

New London Librarium

Christ has no body but yours,
No hands, no feet on earth but yours,
Yours are the eyes with which he looks with
Compassion on this world,
Yours are the feet with which he walks to do good,
Yours are the hands, with which he blesses all the world.
Yours are the hands, yours are the feet,
Yours are the eyes, you are his body.
Christ has no body now but yours,
No hands, no feet on earth but yours,
Yours are the eyes
with which he looks on this world with compassion.
Christ has no body now on earth but yours.

St. Teresa of Avila

Contents

Preface	xi
Introduction	xxi
Suor Maria Barbagallo Work in a Troubled World	25
Argentina Missions for Dignity and Decency	81
Central America and Mexico Standing with the Poor	107
Brazil Churches of People, Churches of Brick	153
Sister Lucy Panettieri Walking on Sacred Ground	197
Swaziland Love and Death	219
Acknowledgments	261
About Sister Barbara Staley	263
About Glenn Alan Cheney	265

Preface

Women religious first caught my attention in 1980 when Maryknoll Sisters Maura Clarke and Ita Ford, Ursuline Sister Dorothy Kazel, and Lay Missionary Jean Donovan were abducted, beaten, raped, and murdered in El Salvador. High-ranking officers in the U.S.-backed Salvadoran military had planned and ordered the murders, and soldiers had carried it out. The American government's response was less than sympathetic. President Jimmy Carter suspended military aid to El Salvador, but not for long. Jeanne Kirkpatrick, foreign policy advisor to president-elect Ronal Reagan, offered one of the most cruel and ignorant statements ever uttered by someone of governmental authority. She said, "The nuns were not just nuns; the nuns were political activists."

I got to thinking about nuns, something I hadn't really done before. I wasn't Catholic, and nuns had never entered my life. For reasons I don't know, I carried the common stereotype of elderly grade-school teachers in black and white habits who enforced discipline with a twelve-inch ruler. When not rapping a kid across the knuckles, they were harping on penmanship or papal history. They spent the rest of their days cloistered in prayer.

But Sisters Maura, Ita, and Dorothy were not in Central America to impose Catholic values on grade-schoolers. I didn't know exactly what they were doing in El Salvador, nor was I able to find out from press reports. I figured it had something to do with helping the poor, and not just with prayer. They were indeed "activists," but where would one draw a line between "activism" and "political activism" and, for that matter, "Catholic activism"? Under the military regimes of Central America, acts in defense of the poor were acts against the interests of the wealthy elite. Such activism was, by definition, political. And politics in Central America was a dangerous pursuit.

Central America wasn't a place I would have expected to find nuns engaged in dangerous activities. But there they were, doing what they felt called to do, be it political, be it religious, or be it something else, some overlap of the two, some new kind of politics or religion, something beyond my previous understanding. I was intrigued by this new area of personal ignorance.

I started looking into the work of nuns. I found out that

Preface

nuns are one thing, sisters another. The former was a term more for cloistered women religious dedicated to prayer. The latter was better applied to women religious following a vocation that took them into a world where they felt compelled to not just worship but serve their God as he asked them to do in the Gospel. I heard about sisters working with abused women in the slums of Phnom Penh, with people who earned their living off a municipal garbage dump, with landless workers in the interior of Brazil, with victims of the war in Congo, with refugees in South Sudan, with survivors of the genocide in East Timor. These were women working in places where few men would dare go, women armed with nothing more than love and faith.

When I heard about a Brazilian sister in Amazonia under constant death threats, I decided to go there. I met Irmã Leonora Brunetto, of the Brazilian congregation Sisters of the Immaculate Heart of Mary. Sixty-seven years old, she'd been in the trenches of humanitarian struggles for some forty years. She was in Terra Nova do Norte, a town that had been uninhabited jungle just a generation earlier. It was effectively lawless, beyond the range of the federal government, under the control of local police who could be hired to kill. By the time I got there, the rainforest was gone, the land was drying up, and a few individuals were claiming tens of thousands of acres without really owning any of it. Thousands of landless people camped outside these farms for years, waiting for plots they were entitled to under Brazil's land redistribution plan. Slavery was common. Murders of peasants went unpunished. The system of justice wasn't working. The environment was in a death spiral. Irmã Leonora was dealing with all of these problems, and though many people loved her, a few—those with land, money, or power—wanted to see her dead. Once she spent three days fleeing pistoleiros intent on killing her. When I finally asked her if she believed God was going to stop the bullets from finding her, she said, with confident certainty, "No."

I left Terra Nova a different person. I'd never seen a place with so many problems, nor had I ever met anyone with such courage and determination. I'd never known anyone who worked so hard and had such an intimate, loving relationship with thousands of impoverished and outcast people. When I finally wiped away my tears, I managed to write a short book with a title that couldn't be any shorter than Promised Land: A nun's struggle against landlessness, lawlessness, slavery, poverty, corruption, injustice, and environmental devastation in Amazonia.

My plan was to write a series of short books about sisters working under difficult or dangerous circumstances, then combine the books into a full-length book. The work of the sisters would serve as a literary device for writing about the general situation in a given place. Because they are are often at the center of so many crucial problems, the work of sisters often touches on a nation's history, culture, economy, and political situation. It was an interesting way to frame a book.

It was hard to find these sisters. They were often beyond the reach of email, and even if not, they weren't the type to

Preface

spend much time at a computer. And if I managed to find them and get a message to them, they usually had more important concerns than me. And if they did have time to respond, their message was that their situations were too complicated and too dangerous to have me there adding to the difficulties.

Then I heard about some sisters in the outback of Swaziland, which I was hard put to find on a map. I fired off an email to the New York office of their congregation, the Missionary Sisters of the Sacred Heart of Jesus, also known as The Cabrini Sisters, named after their patron Saint, Francesca Xavier Cabrini. To my surprise, within an hour I got a response from Sister Barbara Staley, one of the sisters in Swaziland, except she happened to be in Rome at the moment. Sister Barbara, not one to delay action, invited me to Swaziland.

So I went. I arrived at the parched and, at the time, rather chilly outpost called St. Phillip's. Cabrini Sisters had been administering the place for over thirty years. Sister Barbara and Sister Diane DalleMolle had been there for about ten. They'd arrived just as the region was besieged by pandemic HIV. One in three people carried the virus. Tuberculosis was rampant. Whole families were dying. Orphans were left without parents or any other relatives. Houses were falling apart. The economy was comatose. Lethal snakes and black magic were common. The king of Swaziland couldn't care less. For ten years Sister Barbara and Sister Diane had been struggling against a rising flood of misery, working 18 hours a day to get treatment for AIDS patients, food for decimated families, shelter for scores of orphans. They were driving around in rattly-bang cars, drinking cloudy water from dubious sources, dealing with people too shy to talk to them, trying to raise money for a clinic and an orphanage, running all over trying to save bodies and souls. For that decade, a few moments of rest might well mean letting someone die. By the time I arrived, the worst of the worst had passed. For the first time, the two sisters had a few moments to talk about everything they'd been through, everything they'd gotten shotcomings.

Once again, I left the scene in tears, traumatized by the scope of the problems, the warmth of a devastated people, and the heroic efforts of two women who wouldn't let impossibility stop them. I wrote another short book, Love and Death in the Kingdom of Swaziland. It was a good title. It summarized the situation I'd witnessed—an unfathomable amount of love applied against an epidemic so serious it threatened the existence of a nation.

A couple of years later, Sister Barbara was elected General Superior of her Congregation. She packed a decade of Swaziland into her heart and everything else she owned into a single suitcase, and off to Rome she flew. She hit the ground running—that's the only speed she goes—and before long she contacted me to suggest a book about Cabrini sisters in various countries. I would have to go to the slums of Buenos Aires, the inner cities and impoverished interior of Brazil, the struggling schools and traumatic past of Managua, the collapsing social web of Guatemala City, and the gang-controlled desert town of

Preface

Altar, Mexico. Each place was a story of not just sisters but the world of troubles around them.

Sister Barbara warned me that interviews might be a little difficult. Cabrini Sisters might be bold and courageous in their actions, but in conversation, they were more likely to hide their candles than blow their horns. By their missionary nature, she said, Cabrini Sisters tend to see themselves as less important than the people they work with. They are modest about their accomplishments. On top of that, their lives are often beyond most people's experience. How were they going to talk about living through wars and earthquakes, epidemics and pandemic crime, dark slums and distant villages, dictators and gang lords, the travails of the most downtrodden people in the world? On top of that, there was their faith, their vocation, and the Cabrini charism. How was a secular humanist with Presbyterian roots going to understand things that sisters themselves spend a lifetime trying to understand?

The answer to that last question is, Not very well. Yet that very question—that mysterious place where faith, vocation, charism, and God meet—was the one that intrigued me most. I didn't expect to find an answer, but I did hope to come closer to one.

At each community I visited, at least one sister would ask me about my faith or religious convictions. (Curiously, it was always during a meal.) The reader of this book may have similar thoughts, so I might as well confess. I believe that Jesus had the best idea anyone has ever come up with in the history of civilization—that idea of living with goodwill (or call it love), of revering the principles of forgiveness and generosity, of defending peace, avoiding materialism, and living by the so-called Golden Rule. It is by faith and faith alone (because I cannot rationalize it with logic or evidence) that I believe that the overarching idea expressed in the Sermon on the Mount is enough to make heaven on earth a possibility. Likewise, the absence of that most civil idea would leave us back in the jungle. Thus I try to live my life, falling miserably short but always striving in that direction. That said, I admit my difficulty in believing that Jesus was a God. And as for the other God, well, I just don't know how we can know anything about Him (or Her, or even Them or It, or even, arguably, Us). The Bible is a beautiful piece of literature and a very interesting angle on history, and it's chock-full of good moral advice. Also questionable moral advice. I just don't know how to accept it as a font of absolute Truth. My faith is in something else, something I don't understand any better than I understand God.

None of the sisters ever argued with me or tried to convince me otherwise, not even a little. We knew (or at least I knew) we shared a set of fundamental values. We were working for the same cause. The big difference was their unfathomable faith, that mysterious place where they could see and I couldn't. They saw light where I saw only foggy dark.

In my search for a better understanding of God and the good, I could not deny one thing: The Missionary Sisters of the Sacred Heart of Jesus, in the tradition of Mother Cabrini, were accomplishing the impossible. Though in most cases at an age where most people would retire, these women were working harder than anyone I've ever known. They lived under conditions that put them close to the poorest of the poor. They put themselves in harm's way to prevent harm to others. They loved—truly loved—everyone. That level of love is, to me, something like miraculous. The Missionary Sisters of the Sacred Heart were using love to accomplish miracles, and that's something I will be thinking about for a long, long time.

GLENN ALAN CHENEY
HANOVER, CONN.

Introduction

It has been a hundred years since Saint Frances Xavier Cabrini ended her mission on earth. She is the prototype and exemplar of what it means to be a Missionary of the Sacred Heart of Jesus. Her life, completely given to the Heart of Jesus, inspired her contemporaries and has inspired countless others during these past hundred years.

Cabrini was a woman ahead of her time, and she had the courage of a lion. She never let hardships stop her from following God's will. She was, as St. Teresa of Avila expressed it so well, Christ's hands on earth and the eyes through which He looked on the world with compassion.

Not unlike immigrants today, Mother Cabrini was greeted with hostility in New York, and she received little support from the local Church. This did not deter her. With single-minded determination, she opened orphanages for children who had nowhere else to grow up. She established schools for those who had nowhere else to learn. She founded hospitals to care for those who had nowhere else to turn. She visited prisoners in Sing Sing, descended into the mines of Colorado to minister to miners laboring under inhuman conditions, and nursed victims of yellow fever in New Orleans. She swung a pick-axe to dig the foundation of a church. She performed miracles.

Mother Cabrini was a passenger on a train from Denver to New Orleans when it was assaulted by bandits. A bullet missed her head by inches. In Nicaragua she crossed a rainforest by a small riverboat. She crossed the Andes for days on the back of a mule, nearly dying when the mule lost its footing and slid down an icy embankment. Though terrified of water after nearly drowning in her childhood, she crossed the Atlantic Ocean more than twenty-five times. On a couple of those trips the ship traversed storms so severe that all passengers thought their end had come. It was Mother Cabrini who, pushing past her own fear, consoled and encouraged the others to be brave and to trust in the Providence of God. She almost boarded the *Titanic* for its maiden voyage, but her plans changed at the last minute.

How did this woman accomplish so much? She was raised in a small town and led a sheltered childhood. Until the age of thirty she never traveled more than ten miles from home. What motivated Mother Cabrini to face her fears, leave her

Introduction

home, and travel the world, doing the impossible again and again and again? It was really very simple. She was driven and strengthened by her love of God and of people. With the strength of God in her hands and spirit, Mother Cabrini was able to act passionately and swiftly. But still she said she could never keep up with Jesus' desire to be known in the world. As such, with her spirit, faith, strength, and determination, Mother Cabrini exemplifies the meaning of being a Missionary of the Sacred Heart of Jesus. This is the legacy she left us.

The legacy continues. This book is an effort to share the heroic stories of sisters and lay partners in mission, living and dead, who have followed in Mother Cabrini's footsteps. Unfortunately, time and space allow us only to share a few of these stories. I wish that we could have written biographies of so many more women on whose shoulders the Missionary Sisters of the Sacred Heart of today stand. So many sisters and lay partners in mission have gone about their lives and worked selflessly to give of themselves as expression of their commitment to Christ.

I hope that the brief biographies presented here, which represent only a small sample of the lives of so many others, capture your interest and imagination as they did mine. The lives and self-giving of the women portrayed here leave me in awe about the reality of the saints who live among us. Their lives—and the lives they symbolize—encourage me to stay on my own journey of Faith and to do what I can to help create

God's heavenly reign in the here and now.

As we move into the next hundred years, my hope is that more women will be daring enough to give themselves completely to the Heart of Jesus as Missionaries of the Sacred Heart. I pray that all who read this be bold enough to give themselves to others without considering the cost, without expecting any return, no matter what their stature in life, no matter what their religion or nationality. Saint Cabrini understood that the "world is too small." She could not limit charity to one group, nor could she move fast enough to keep pace with God's call to show love to others. From her we learn, and thus we live. May all of us love with the passion and urgency of our saint and founder, Mother Frances Cabrini. We are her hands on earth.

SR. BARBARA STALEY, MSC
CODOGNO, ITALY

Madre Maria Barbagallo

Work in a Troubled World

To understand why Suor Maria Barbagallo got pulled from Nicaragua not long after the Sandinistas took Managua, and how events there led to her work as General Superior, and how half a century of religious life gradually built into a deeper understanding of the meaning of religious life, we have to go back to the dark days that led up to World War II in Europe. Mussolini came to power in 1922 on an unabashedly pro-fascism, anti-socialism platform. In February, 1929, Italy granted independence and autonomy to the Vatican City State, ensuring Catholic support of the National Fascist party. Eight months later, the American stock market collapsed, not only causing a depression in Europe but bringing into question the viability of capitalism in the face of a new economic system called communism. In 1934, the German Reischtag burned, leading to the political chaos from which Adolph Hitler rose to power. Within a year, civil war broke out in Spain, pitting fascist Republicans against socialist Nationalists. In 1939, Hitler invaded Poland, and Mussolini declared Italy's alliance with the Nazis. It was a strange and threatening world to grow up in, but none of it bothered Maria Barbagallo. She was four.

The developments bothered Maria's father, however. A banker of somewhat aristocratic birth and intellectual tendencies, he wrote scathing essays on the evils of fascism. Mussolini put up with no such opposition, not at any level, not on any scale. He had Mr. Barbagallo fired. Barbagallo and his wife, a practical woman of less than aristocratic birth, and five children moved to Sicily to be near his family. His reputation followed him, however, and the Sicilian welcome was less than warm. To get rations during the war, Mrs. Barbagallo secretly joined the Fascist party. In school, the children had to sing songs praising the party. When Mr. Barbagallo's father died, he left nothing for the son who had disappointed him with his poverty, his politics, and his poor choice of wife. The son soon died of tuberculosis aggravated by, Maria says, terminal sadness and the stress of watching the world fall apart.

After the war, the family moved back to Rome. Maria Barbagallo joined a church organization called Catholic Action. She earned a teaching certificate and was about twenty when she was leading a group of teens. They had a lot of fun. It was a good time to be young in Italy. The war was over and life was changing. The country was rebuilt. Food was more available. Television was bringing culture from other countries. Elvis

Work in a Troubled World

Presley showed everyone a new way to dance. Maria liked to go out and dance. She was a bit of a diavoletta, a little devil, not really bad but maybe sometimes swept up in the exuberance of youth, going out at night, listening to jazz and dancing the cha-cha-cha a little later into the evening than a young lady should.

The cultural changes were touching the Church as well. Fewer young people were interested in Catholic Action. The vocation to monasteries and convents was withering, too. Liberal ideas from the French Church were creeping into Italy and Spain, but monks and nuns still lived in a parallel world that seemed, to Maria, stuck in medieval times. She herself had notions of becoming a nun. The possibility crossed her mind, anyway, but it didn't stop there. She could see herself dedicating her life to the service of God, but who wants to be a nun, cloistered and silent, isolated from the world, from jazz and dancing, doing nothing but praying and occasionally smacking a ruler across the knuckles of a grade-schooler? Not Maria Barbagallo.

Maria's vocation, for the moment, was her Catholic Action group. To keep her kids engaged, she had to make it fun. She wrote a play for the group. They put it on, and it was a big success—so big that they were invited to give a performance at the Roman convent of the Missionary Sisters of the Sacred Heart of Jesus, also known as the Cabrini Sisters, also abbreviated as "MSC" for the Latin Missionararum a Sacro Corde.

Maria and her cast of young thespians were a bit nervous about staying with nuns. Nuns were respected, certainly, but weren't seen as a whole lot of fun. One had to be careful around them. They liked things clean and quiet, and they believed in the importance of discipline. A convent wasn't going to be an easy fit for Maria and a bunch of teenagers.

The group showed up at the convent. To their surprise, the Sisters were kind, humble, human, and solicitous, and of course their convent was spotless. They didn't seem cloistered or disciplinary. They offered the group whatever they needed—pencils, paper, whatever. They didn't march the kids to the laundry tank to wash their dirty clothes. They collected the clothes and returned them clean, dry, and folded. When the kids came back from a jaunt one rainy day, they forgot themselves and let their umbrellas drip all over the foyer floor. Maria was sure they were in for some discipline. But the Sisters said not to worry, they'd clean it up.

These were nuns unlike any she'd ever known. Maria went to the Mother Superior and asked how a person would join such a congregation. Not that she wanted to! She was just curious. The Superior explained. Another Sister gave her some books. Maria took them home. She was a big reader, loved books, consumed them like buttered popcorn. Almost a year later the Sister called to talk about the books. It wasn't a recruitment call. It was just to talk about books and ideas. That went on for a while—Maria reading, the Cabrini Sister calling to chat, then sending more books. They talked about the impossible accomplishments of Mother Francesca Cabrini, all the schools and hospitals she had founded in New York, New Orleans,

Work in a Troubled World

Chicago, Seattle, Nicaragua, Panama, Argentina, France, Spain, Italy, her travels to all those places, her 24 trips across the Atlantic, her crossing the Andes on a mule. This was the mission of the Cabrini Sisters—to go wherever the poor and downtrodden needed help and to do whatever was necessary even if impossible. This was not the surreal medieval life of cloistered nuns. It was adventure, exploration, the conversion of Christian principles into earthly action. It appealed very much to Maria. Her family didn't like the idea of her giving her life to the Church, so she prepared for it in secret. She was 24 when she signed up.

She figured she'd be on her way overseas in a week or two. But becoming a Cabrini Sister isn't like joining the army. It doesn't happen overnight. It's a process that can take a decade or more. Adventure and social work were only the visible side of the religious life. The deeper inner side were every bit as important but ever so much more difficult to discern.

Step one was the novitiate. Maria—as of her entry to the novitiate, she was Suor (Sister) Maria—and twelve other young women learned about the implications and obligations of a vow of obedience, chastity, and poverty. They began to learn the extent and depth of the MSC mission. It involved a study of the Congregational charism—that indefinable grace, that gift of the spirit of God that is often given to a few leaders, that motivation that impels a person to go forth in mission. In the case of St. Frances Cabrini, her motivation was the love for Jesus and the passion for all her Sisters to be bearers of the love of the Sacred

29

Heart of Jesus. The Cabrini charism is a way of life and a way of loving modeled after Jesus' love, that generous and total giving of the self to others. Discerning the Cabrini charism is a lifetime pursuit. For Suor Maria and the Sisters who joined her in the novitiate, this discernment began with a search for an understanding of the primacy of God in the world, an analysis of the sacramental life. It also involved housecleaning, dishwashing, and cooking. They spent most of their time in silence. Early each morning they practiced solitary prayer. Then church. Then chores. All without speaking except during designated times, one of which was known as "recreation."

For Suor Maria, recreation was the best time of the day. She loved to hear the older Sisters talk about their lives and missions. World War II was still on their minds, and the Spanish Sisters remembered the Civil War in their country. When fascism and German troops reigned over Italy, the Cabrini Sisters tried to stay out of the fray. War wasn't their mission. But it simply wasn't possible to avoid it. They hid three fugitive Jews in Rome, and they hid an American Sister—technically an enemy of Italy—at their house in Genoa until an American soldier helped her leave Italy. Sisters became smugglers as they took trips into the countryside and returned with contraband crops under their habits. Often they had to go without food so they had a little something for their orphans. By the time the Allies fought their way to Rome, the Sisters were so weak they could barely stand up.

During these recreation periods at the novitiate, the

Work in a Troubled World

Spanish Sisters had horrific tales of atrocities in Spain. Franco had supported the Church, but he was also overthrowing an elected government, and his Republican forces were guilty of unrestrained massacres and torture. The socialists that opposed him were, in the model of Soviet Stalinism, opposed to religion, and their Nationalist forces were guilty of burning Catholic convents, schools, and hospitals. With dubious reason, the Church sided with the Republicans. They seemed safer than the Socialists, who were unabashedly anti-religion. Priests and teachers were murdered, orphans were moved from Catholic orphanages to government agencies, and some of the MSC Sisters spent time in Nationalist prisons. In one anecdote, a Sister told of three Spanish Sisters who were arrested. A female guard asked why they didn't leave their Congregation and have a little fun in life. They replied that they were having plenty of fun in life by helping and loving people. They told the guard that, doing what she was doing, she was the one without fun in life.

These were tense times not just for the world but for the Church. Society was loosening up. The Cold War kept enemies at the brink of nuclear holocaust. The Soviet Union was suppressing religion, punishing writers and thinkers, and maintaining its "gulag" of concentration camps. In 1951, after 25 years of missionary work, the MSC pulled out of China to escape suppression under Mao. In most of the smaller countries of the world, tinpot dictators were using brutal force to sustain an economic divide between a wealthy elite and great masses of poor. Gandhi was dead but his fame and philosophy were not. Martin Luther King was planting Gandhian ideas of human rights and passive resistance in the United States. French writers and theologians were starting to rethink the mission of the Church.

The Church at that time was concerned less with the poor than with guiding people into faith and eventually into heaven. To the poor, the Church offered spiritual solace and the promise of posthumous reward for their toil, suffering, and patience on earth. The MSCs, on the other hand, were very much out in the field, helping those whom society had not valued. But still, strategically, the furthering of MSC institutions, such as schools and hospitals, sometimes took precedence over the needs and potentials of the individuals within it. The missionary charism—the institutional vision—was focused more on itself than on a world in change. Vocations and missions were directed more toward strengthening the institutions than keeping up with the world. Spirituality was focused on sacrifice and obedience. The governance of the Institute was concentrated in the hands of the General Superior rather than shared by all the Sisters.

In the novitiate there was little talk of serving the poor in any but the traditional ways of establishing schools and hospitals. Politics was not discussed, and notions of changing the orientation of the Church never penetrated the Convent walls—at least not in Italy. In the United States, MSC Sisters were a little more uppity and independent, smuggling newspapers and books into their community houses. They were a little more

Work in a Troubled World

ready for what was coming.

What was coming was the Second Vatican Council, known as Vatican II. It started under Pope John XIII, who wanted to, in his words, open the windows of the Church and let in some fresh air. The Council started in 1962 and concluded in 1965 under the more conservative Pope Paul VI. Among other things, it called for a turning of the Church toward the needs of people. Service to God was suddenly being interpreted as service to people. After centuries of saying Mass in Latin, the Church returned to speaking to the faithful in their local languages. Priests could face the faithful rather than the altar while celebrating mass. And congregations of men and women religious were asked to loosen up a bit, to become more democratic and participatory, and to focus their efforts on the needs of the modern world.

It was a shock to Suor Maria and other MSCs. They hadn't even known the Council was happening, let alone what direction it was going. Apparently their General Superior, Sister Valentina, knew something about it, but to Sisters in Italy and most other parts of the world, it was a complete and confusing surprise. Some Sisters accepted the changes while others resisted. Looking back on it today, Suor Maria says it was a miracle—a miracle attributable to Mother Cabrini—that the congregation didn't rupture and split in two.

The Congregation did not rupture. It changed. Silence was replaced with a call to discuss things. The big convents were broken into smaller units where Sisters could get to know each other and develop deeper and more human relationships. Sisters were encouraged to pursue more education. Mature integration of spirit, emotions, intellect, and physical well-being became part of their mission. They were encouraged to hash things out, to return to the roots of the Mother Cabrini charism and its mission. In the future, they would all participate in the election of General Superiors.

But other things didn't change, at least not much. Suor Maria was upset to see that women religious in many congregations were treated like second-class Catholic workers. Too many of them were serving far below the potential of their talents and capacities. In Africa, India, and Latin America, they were often relegated to nothing higher than serving priests, not much more than cheap labor. This was less true among the MSCs but nonetheless somewhat true. She thought Cabrini Sisters should be a stronger force in spiritual, community, and apostolic life—not the same as priests, but with a more influential role and more options for applying their creativity and their special capacity to understand the world and its people, to help the Church exercise love, mercy, and compassion.

But at that stage of her vocation, pushing for such change was far beyond her mission. The Congregation sent her to Rome to finish her degree in psychology. And not long after she received her Bachelor's degree, she was informed how she was to put it to use. She was going to Guatemala to serve as director of a novitiate.

* * *

Work in a Troubled World

Suor Maria arrived in Managua in September of 1974 with a group of novices from Europe. Their welcome to sunny, tropical Nicaragua was a bad lashing by the tail of Hurricane Fifi, one of the deadliest storms ever to hit Central America. It passed just north of Managua, dropping over 14 inches of rain in four days. Winds reached 130 miles per hour. In Honduras, several thousand people died as whole towns were washed away by waves and landslides. In Managua the winds howled maniacally and rain thundered down. The Sisters were terrified by the sound and the violence of it. Rain leaked in through the roof. Mold lay siege to shoes, luggage, and clothes.

Managua suffered less than other places, but the city had barely begun to pull itself up from a worse disaster of an earthquake back in December of 1972. Fifty thousand people died in the quake, and the center of the city still lay in ruins. The fault line, in fact, ran right under an MSC school, which the congregation had just finished rebuilding. The building collapsed, as did Nicaraguans' faith in their government. The oligarchic military regime of Anastasio Somoza showed little concern for the suffering of its people or the condition of its capital. Foreign aid ended up financing the rebuilding of the houses of only the elite. Virtually nothing was done for the poor. The vast majority of Nicaraguans, mired in hopeless poverty even in the best of times, had never liked Somoza very much. After the disdain he showed them following the earthquake, almost everyone decided they didn't like him at all. An old insurgency began to gather strength in the more inaccessible corners of the country, coalescing into the Frente Sandinista de Liberación Nacional. The Sandinistas were brutally suppressed by Somoza's Guardia Nacional but never stamped out. The brunt of the brutality fell on civilians suspected of supporting the Sandinistas.

The situation in Nicaragua was in many ways quite like that of the rest of Central America—politically, economically, and tectonically shaky. Guatemala had a long history of military governments suppressing the poor, especially the indigenous population. The governments of Honduras and El Salvador were also contending with guerrilla movements. In these agrarian countries, most of the arable land was in the hands of a few families. Social assistance for the poor was nonexistent.

So when Suor Maria arrived in Guatemala City, the first thing she had to do was learn that she wasn't in Italy anymore. She took a six-week course organized by the Confederatión Csribeaña y Latinoamericana de Religiosas/os (CLAR). She joined 150 participants from 18 countries.

It was here that Suor Maria Barbagallo felt her true self born, a self turned to both humanity and God. She came to understand so much about the problems of the world, the vocation to reach out to the poor, and the necessity of Sisters inserting themselves into the realm and reality of poverty. The conference presented the reality of Latin America—the military governments, the masses of poor, the social injustice, the starvation wages, the general illiteracy, the marginalization of indigenous peoples—

Work in a Troubled World

as it really was. It knitted together those realities in the light of Vatican II and another milestone document that reflected realities in Latin America, a controversial pronouncement issued by the Medellin Conference.

The Medellin Conference was held by Latin American Bishops in 1968. It took Vatican II a step further, applying its human orientation to the situation of humans in Latin America. The conference resolved that under the principles of Vatican II, the Church—at least in Latin America—should "opt for the poor." This meant directing Church efforts to teaching people to read and to realize that God did not want them to live in poverty or under oppression. The new direction was a threat to established governments and socio-economic disparity. It was also indirect moral support for Marxist movements. It quickly became a source of contention and, soon, conflict. Liberation theology extended the Medellin principles even further into the principles of Marxism. In fact, communist parties in Central America openly supported the CLAR mission, which inevitably led to suspicions that communism and the Church were suspiciously similar.

One lesson taught was that the Church was by no means innocent. Centuries before, the Church had cooperated with the colonization of the Americas. It had sanctioned slavery, supported the powers that were, and forced European values, culture, and religion on indigenous people. It was guilty of pacifying the poor with promises of a better life after life. Elements of that approach to society lived on into the current times. But the times—and the Church—were changing.

Through a formal process they called "theological reflection," the religious in the CLAR organizations asked themselves what God wanted them to do and what the Gospel called on them to do. They took a good, hard look at the sociopolitical reality of Latin America. Seeing reality as it really is became the mandate for all member organizations, and it became the foundation of the orientation course that Suor Maria took. And when they thought about it, much of the work of religious organizations was by all appearances favoring injustice! Their schools were for the elite. Their hospitals were for those who could afford them. Sermons and programs turned a blind eye to obvious problems. When the Jesuits of Latin American took a good look at reality as it was, they realized that virtually every single dictator in Latin America had received a Jesuit education. It was then that the Jesuits committed themselves to social justice.

These were all new concepts to Suor Maria, quite different from the Catholicism that she'd grown up with. But as she learned about the situation in Central America, as she heard of the great masses of poor—the vast majority of the population—being brutally oppressed, even genocidally slaughtered, her eyes opened. She saw a new reality. She understood and accepted the new role of the Church and the new nature of her mission. Under the precepts of Vatican II and the Medellin Conference, MSCs were to be in solidarity with the poor. Solidarity meant living among the poor and living as they did. If the poor lacked

Work in a Troubled World

water, Sisters lacked water. If the poor suffered oppression and injustice, Sisters suffered it, too.

In Central America, that oppression was extreme. People got killed for even speaking about injustice. Carrying a document or poster with the name "Che Guevara" on it was essentially a capital offense. In Nicaragua, one means of execution—of disappearing people so they stayed disappeared—was to take prisoners away by helicopter and drop them into Masaya, an active volcano within sight of Managua.

As director of a novitiate, Maria would be preparing young Sisters to opt for the poor and live in solidarity with them. Sisters would be involved in everything from promoting literacy to resisting injustice to helping the voiceless be heard.

And that meant danger. It meant that Missionary Sisters of the Sacred Heart of Jesus would be working for many (but certainly not all) of the same goals that the guerrillas were fighting for in Nicaragua, Guatemala, El Salvador, and Honduras. Obviously the Church and the guerrillas were employing different strategies—the Church wielding love, the guerrillas wielding guns—but both wanted to free the poor from institutionalized oppression. One major difference was that clergy and religious workers were not armed. They did not and could not fight back. Nor did they live in inaccessible mountain hideouts. Their only defense was the mercy of those in power, a mercy to a great extent based on fear of stirring up an insurrection by abusing the Church too much. Still, priests were often murdered or arrested and never heard from again.

Nuns were considered little different from communist agents undermining the upper class by helping the lower class.

This confusion of Church and communism would become blatant in 1980 when two Maryknoll Sisters, Maura Clarke and Ita Ford, flew into El Salvador from Managua. Ursuline Sister Dorothy Kazen and lay worker Jean Donovan met them at the airport. All four were American citizens. Apparently someone was waiting for them. A military death squad followed them from the airport, abducted them, then beat, raped, and murdered them. Jeane Kirkpatrick, U.S. ambassador to the United Nations, commented, "The nuns were not just nuns; the nuns were political activists...They were political activists on behalf of the Frente [guerrillas]." The notion was as absurd as it was ignorant and cruel, but in a certain way it represented the attitude and opinion of the Reagan administration.

The four women were by no means the only religious murdered by security forces in Central America. In 1977, Padre Rutilio Grande, S.J., was gunned down for advocating liberation theology and working with rural peasants in El Salvador. Óscar Romero, archbishop of El Salvador, was gunned down in 1980 while celebrating mass. Suor Maria knew some of the six Jesuits who were massacred in El Salvador in 1989. Padre Ignacio Ellacuría was one of them. She remembers him as a great theologian who was not afraid to tell the truth about the causes of poverty.

Shortly after Suor Maria arrived in Guatemala, the MSCs and some ten other congregations decided to open and operate a single organization for inter-congregational formation. They called it The International School. The hope was to knit everyone together in their common cause, the option for the poor in the face of economic and governmental oppression.

There was, however, a little theo-pedagogical stress in the school. Some of the congregations were more progressive, others more conservative. Though MSCs are considered a relatively conservative congregation in the United States, in Central America, it was over on the progressive end. While some congregations preferred a more cloistered, silent environment, for example, the MSCs wanted their Sisters to speak at will, to question at will, and to share ideas. It was a school for Sisters, but, in a recent liberalization, a few padres and hermanos served as teachers and advisors. Among them were Italian Franciscans, who certainly leaned hard toward the traditional and conservative. There were many discussions about the correct "formation" of Sisters, whether they had to be squeezed into a mold to learn and accept the special demands of the religious life, or whether more freedom would allow for individual growth. The MSCs were already applying principles of psychology to help guide their novices, but more conservative voices doubted that an integrated psychology would work better than the old methods of institutional spiritualization.

Suor Maria wanted to see full human integration involved in the formation process. She didn't want to see the process oriented around the disposal or denial of supposedly inappropriate human characteristics. She wanted novices and aspirants to understand that they were to bring their whole humanness into their vocation. To live a truly transcendent life for Christ, humanness had to include individuality, intelligence, introspection, free choice, and self-development. She developed those thoughts for courses she taught on religious psycho-pedagogy and related subjects. To prepare, she read what sociologists and theologians from Germany to Argentina had to say about religious missionary life. She came to more truly understand liberation theology and its implications. She learned how to study reality, theologically reflect on it, apply the Gospel to it, and then make pastoral decisions. She came to better understand how faith, charism, vocation, and human growth are all related, and she became more confident in her beliefs.

Over time it became apparent that openness was more productive than restriction. Preventing novices from visiting their families, for example, led to Sisters faking dental appointments so they could sneak off to visit home. Liberty, it turned out, nurtured responsibility, fostered self-actualization, and, in more mundane terms, promoted job satisfaction. Sisters were given all the education they could handle. They were allowed to leave the convent alone. They took trips to the beach. They put on a performance of *Romeo and Juliet*. All of this, even Shakespeare, was new to the Sisters from Central American countries.

In the spirit of Medellin, the basic MSC strategy for working in solidarity with the poor was to form "Christian Base

Work in a Troubled World

Communities." Each would have some kind of pastoral leader who would explain scripture and—most significantly—lead discussions about how scripture related to people's lives in today's socio-political context. This was new in Latin America. In the past, priests had taken care of scripture and Biblical issues, celebrating mass and leading prayer. But the Gospel was not in the hands of the people. For one thing, many couldn't even read it. For another, the Church had always discouraged the uneducated from grappling with theological issues lest they misunderstand. Literacy back then, therefore, was not of special significance. But with the new emphasis on bringing God and Gospel to the people, teaching the poor to read and write was an essential mission. But literacy did not serve the interest of the oligarchy, so the teaching of it was associated with communist subversion. Base community leaders were among those targeted by death squads, unwarranted arrest, and summary imprisonment or disappearance. Helping people understand the Gospel could get a person dropped into a volcano.

People started calling these executed leaders "the new martyrs." Conservative elements in the Church, however, refused to accept violent deaths as martyrdom. Under Church doctrine, martyrs die for issues of faith, not politics. But in Central America, faith and politics were becoming tightly intermingled. When Archbishop Óscar Romero was assassinated in 1980, Pope John Paul II, who strongly opposed communism, refused to consider him a martyr eligible for sainthood. Though Romero's assassination was unquestionably due to his unceasing calls for an end to social, political, and economic injustice, he was not declared a martyr until Pope Francis—a Latin American himself—did so in 2015. This declaration was especially significant because it established that faith demanded political action.

Traveling to other countries—which Maria did a lot, especially between Guatemala and Nicaragua—was difficult and risky. It seemed that all the Latin American military and dictatorial governments were cooperating to suppress travel. Men and women religious had a hard time getting visas. They were considered runners for a communist post office. At airports and border crossing, they were often pulled aside and thoroughly searched. Officials pawed through everything from underwear to Bibles in search of hidden papers or incriminating evidence of cooperation with Marxists. Any printed materials were taken away, maybe even used to justify arrest. It was the same all over Latin America. Treatment at customs at the Buenos Aires airport was about the same as at Managua. Police had blacklists with photographs of nuns, monks, Jesuits, priests, and other alleged subversives. To travel from Guatemala to Nicaragua by land, which Maria and other religious often did in a minivan, required crossing borders between Guatemala and El Salvador, El Salvador and Honduras, Honduras and Nicaragua—all countries with military governments and guerrilla uprisings. Suor Maria thought she was a goner the time she flew into Managua from Guatemala. As soon as she got off the plane, officials took her into a separate room. This was often the first step toward disappearance. They put her in front of a camera, told her to hold a card with a number on it to her chest, told her to turn this way and that as they photographed her from the front and both sides. She felt like a criminal being arrested. But then they let her go.

In 1976 Maria went to Nicaragua with some of her novices for a little vacation on the beach at a little house the MSCs had. They were looking out to sea one evening, appreciating the beauty of the moonlight on the oddly troubled water. Suddenly one of the novices said she was afraid. Something was wrong. She didn't know what it was. The next morning, at 4:00, a phone call came in. Maria was to go to Guatemala City immediately. There had been a terrible earthquake. The city was in ruins. Communication was impossible. No one knew the fate of the MSC Sisters who lived there.

Maria rushed to the airport with one of the novices but was informed that all flights to Guatemala were, of course, cancelled. It would be quite impossible to fly there for the indefinite future. Impossibility, however, had never stopped Mother Cabrini or any Cabrini Sister since. Suor Maria looked and probed and whined and wheedled and asked around and finally sobbed her way onto a military aircraft headed for the disaster zone. At the Guatemala City airport, she found, incredibly, a taxi willing to take her into the city. Along the way, she was astonished at the silence—no traffic, no people, no sounds of life. Everyone had left the city in fear of the aftershocks. The scene was otherworldly, the fronts of buildings lying in the streets, the innards of kitchens and bedrooms exposed. The only people around were looters. Maria arrived at the MSC house. It was a wreck, the outer walls still up but everything inside collapsed. The two Sisters who had remained there rather than go on vacation to Nicaragua were nowhere to be found. It turned out that they had been smart, first standing in doorways rather than running outside, then getting into their pick-up truck and driving to a place where nothing would fall on them. Suor Maria asked around and soon found them sleeping in their truck in a field.

Many of the churches in the city had collapsed. As the Sisters wandered around looking for some kind of church-based rescue operation, they found that all the priests were chiefly concerned with saving their churches, the icons of saints, the holy this and that that lay under the rubble. Evangelical Protestants were thumping their Bibles and telling people that God had wreaked this damage to punish the faithless and unfaithful. The Sisters decided that their own efforts should focus on helping the poor who were now without homes, water, food, or medical care.

The government was of little help. Its main effort seemed to be a propaganda campaign based on the uplifting slogan, Guatemala está de pie!— Guatemala still stands! Except that it didn't. Due to the lack of communication and transportation, people had no idea how wide the destruction was. A Guatemalan Sister from another congregation, having not heard from her family in a distant village, felt compelled to go into the countryside to see how they had fared. She found the rural

Work in a Troubled World

area in ruins, the people suffering terribly with no assistance, or even acknowledgement, from the government. She returned to Guatemala City, and as soon as the television broadcaster was operating, she got herself invited to a talk show. There, in tears, she told everyone what was really happening.

The Conference of Religious of Honduras sent the MSCs an emergency response truck. It didn't have much in the way of medicine or equipment, so Maria and two other Sisters did what they could, which was to raise spirits and give people hope. This was almost as important as the more physical assistance that foreign aid groups were providing. People were terribly depressed, and they had a tendency to believe the evangelicals who were saying that the disaster was God's wrath against them personally for their bad behavior. The Sisters drove around to villages—or rather up to villages thousands of meters higher than the nearly mile-high Guatemala City— sounding a klaxon horn and ringing a bell to announce their arrival. In many cases, the Sisters were the only aid in town, so people came in great, desperate crowds. The Sisters organized prayer groups, held meetings, offered advice, blessed people right and left, and showed movies with a projector that had come with the truck. With no other options, the Sisters slept in the truck for a month, depending on peasants for food, bathing in creeks, and sneaking off to latrines when no one was looking. The Sisters from Central America were a lot more comfortable with this than the sisters from the traditional convents of Italy. But to such situations Cabrini Sisters apply a principle they call transcendence—rising above the expected to do what must be done.

During the weeks following the earthquake, foreign aid poured in. Aid organizations, distrusting the government, provided food, medicine, clothes and such to local religious organizations for distribution. The MSCs were especially appreciated because unlike many other religious groups, it provided assistance to whoever needed it, not just to their own constituents. Maria saw a preacher, a Bible under his arm, thundering that these material goods will not save you, only the word of God will save you!

She told him that when people are starving, food is the word of God.

* * *

As Guatemala rebuilt, Nicaragua teetered on revolution. Somoza's Guardia Nacional was unable to rid the country of the Sandinista front, which was gaining the support of the general population, even the middle class. It was hard for the Church and the MSC to distance themselves from the Sandinistas. Many of the Nicaragua Sisters had family members in prison, in the Frente, or already dead or disappeared. The programs and pursuits of the MSC resembled those of the Sandinista "communists" who were fighting for social justice, an end to the economic disparity between upper and lower classes, the general improvement of the plight of the poor. All of this is

Work in a Troubled World

part of the social teachings of the Church and the model given by Jesus in the Gospels. At the same time, the Vatican was uneasy with any association with Marxists. Pope John Paul II, a Pole who had grown up under a communist, Soviet-controlled government, was vehemently opposed to communism and distrustful of any uprising that espoused Marxism even if its objectives looked a lot like the Church's. Neither the Church nor Maria Barbagallo ever espoused the violence of armed revolution, but she knew what the MSCs were dealing with. Her base community leaders were indirectly resisting the social structures that were oppressing the poor. The people whom the MSCs helped were helping the Sandinistas, and the government was utterly and blatantly opposed to any efforts to empower the poor or powerless.

In January of 1978, Pedro Joaquín Chamorro Cardenal, the editor of the left-leaning Managua newspaper, La Prensa, was killed by Somozistas. Riots broke out, more of the middle class called for Somoza to step down, and the Sandinistas gained strength. For months the imminent violence was on everyone's mind and in every conversation. But the oppression worsened, and extensive cruelty held off any progress by the Sandinistas. Everyone was walking on eggs to avoid trouble. They were hoping for change but afraid of the reality of a revolution—the bloodshed and the questionable outcome. An earlier regional director of the MSCs, Victoria de Solar, had always wanted her Sisters to help calm the population, to keep the young from getting involved with the Sandinistas and getting killed by the Guardia Nacional. She was also rather fearful of the real results of a Marxist revolution. Archbishop Miguel Obando y Bravo was also urging congregations to try to stay out of the fray. He was distrustful of liberation theology, but he also wrote commentaries for the archdiocese newspaper that were highly critical of the corruption of the Somoza regime and the abuses of the Guardia Nacional. He was, in fact, so critical that Somozistas referred to him as "Comandante Miguel," as if he were an armed guerrilla.

But it was hard for Cabrini Sisters to stay neutral. When Suor Maria became head of the Congregation's Central America Region in 1978, she knew that neutrality was both necessary and impossible. The MSCs could not fulfill their mission without helping the very people who sided with the Sandinistas. Every day a Nicaraguan Sister would tell Suor Maria that she had a brother or a cousin or a friend who had been arrested, murdered, or disappeared. One had a brother who was in the mountains with the Sandinistas. At the same time, the older Nicaraguan Sisters, who tended to come from the upper class, warned that the younger Sisters, who were often from poor families, were Sandinista sympathizers. So there was stress inside the MSC Congregation just as there was stress between the Vatican and the religious in the socio-political trenches of Central America.

But how could Suor Maria remain neutral when one of her younger Sisters, Juanita, came to tell her that her brother had been arrested? He and a number of others were stuffed into a stifling basement room that was serving as an ad hoc prison.

Work in a Troubled World

They were there only until they could be taken out, tortured for information, then disappeared. They had neither sanitation facility nor food. Families had to bring them food, and in her family, Juanita was the one to take it because perhaps her Sisterhood put her at a little less risk than someone else. Hermana Juanita asked Suor Maria if she and another Sister could take food for her brother and others. With trepidation, Sister Maria told them to go ahead. But on one visit, the brother said that he and some others were working on a plan to escape. They had managed to pry open a little window and get the attention of a construction worker outside. The worker understood that the prisoners weren't in there for any real crimes. He agreed to help. He was going to return with something they could use to rip open the window. But they needed Sister Juanita's help. They needed her to get a car and wait at a certain spot. Juanita went to Suor Maria and explained the situation. Suor Maria knew how serious it was—serious because if the young man didn't get out, he was going to die a horrific death. Serious because if Hermana Juanita got caught, she'd be destined to the same fate. Serious because it would reflect on the whole MSC operation in Nicaragua if not all of Central America—and not just the MSCs but every other religious person and organization. But those were all maybe's while the brother's death was a certainty.

The situation was a moral, political and theological conundrum—a trial-by-fire lesson that was preparing Suor Maria for many difficult decisions she would have to make in the course of a long religious life. Should she sacrifice an individual for the good of the Congregation? Should the safety of scores of other people override the demise of one? Should one ignore the present in deference to the future? How responsible is a Cabrini Sister for the life of a person she doesn't really even know? And should she prevent a young Sister from risking her life to help a family member?

Suor Maria could not give permission, but she also declined to say no. Juanita and her friend took a car to the appointed place. They waited. Time passed. No brother. They left. They went back the next day. Waited. Waited. Nothing. They did this for a week until they got word that the escape would not be possible. Suor Maria was secretly—and uneasily—relieved. Things could have gone terribly worse, with Juanita and her fellow Sister arrested, raped, tortured, and killed after implicating the MSCs. But the brother was still under arrest, which was not something to be glad about. There was really nothing to be glad about in those tense and terrible days.

But within a week, as the Sisters sat eating at the Cabrini community house, they heard a knock on the door. It scared them breathless. They remembered the last time there was a knock on the door after dark. That time, it was three Sandinistas. They demanded that Maria and another Sister, a nurse, come with them. The Sisters asked why. The men wouldn't say. Nor would they let the Sisters refuse. So they went. The Sandinistas took them to a place that was full of severely wounded young men, guerrillas down from the mountains. They had open wounds, infections, limbs missing, limbs in need of amputation. Maria

Work in a Troubled World

and the nurse did what they could but had to leave the next morning.

But this time the knock on the door wasn't Sandinistas. It was Juanita's brother, scratched, bleeding, and filthy. He'd been in a tunnel for the past week and hadn't eaten anything in all that time. He washed quickly, used the bathroom, ate a little something, and ran off lest he get caught and condemn the whole congregation. They never heard from him again until after the revolution.

MSC Sisters with training in nursing often went into poor neighborhoods to help wounded people. This was quite illegal and could have gotten them killed. They had to lie their way past roadblocks and gauntlets of soldiers with machine guns. Sister Flora worked as a kind of spy, going alone into neighborhoods on supposed missions of catechism but really to see where help was needed. Then nurses would come later.

Suor Maria should have felt fear in those days, she knew later. She and every other Sister just assumed that they'd probably meet a violent death. But Maria was oddly—and, she knew later, foolishly—at ease with this. Such is the effect of faith and mission. Her fears were only for others, her people in the field, from Sisters to base community workers to young people who believed the call of the Gospel and were so bold and foolish and faithful as to act on it. She was living in Managua but traveling in cars, trucks, buses, vans, and motorcycles to mountain villages and city slums. It was hardly what she had imagined when she decided to become a Missionary Sister of the Sacred Heart, but it was extremely satisfying. Extremely transcending. She was fully using her considerable capacity for hard work, compassion, rational decisions, and creativity.

Meanwhile, she was losing Sisters. Some, especially the ones from Spain, were afraid to stay in a country increasingly torn by violence between a ruthless government and desperate leftists. It was too reminiscent of the civil war in their own country, and they didn't like the indirect support of Marxists. As the violence worsened, the ambassadors of Italy, Spain, Argentina, Brazil, and other countries were all very helpful in getting religious out of the country.

But most stayed. Their mission had never been so important.

In July of 1979, Suor Maria was called to Rome for a conference. But no sooner had she arrived than she heard that the uprising was really flaring up. The Sandinistas were approaching Managua. Somoza was bombing his own capital city. Maria took the next plane back but had to land in Guatemala City. A few days later—July 19, 1979—the war was being fought in the streets of Managua. Maria went back to the Guatemala City airport the next day, just to find out when there might be a flight. At the ticket counter an attendant asked her if she was crazy. There was a war. The communists were killing everybody. And it didn't matter whether she was crazy or not, there were no flights to Managua whatsoever. But Suor Maria asked around, sobbed here and there, begged and pleaded, finally found a small foreign aid aircraft that was taking some soldiers and civilians to Managua. The Sisters back in the

Work in a Troubled World

novitiate had no idea that she was doing this. She hadn't left with luggage, just a passport and enough money for a ticket. They expected her to come home. They didn't know whether she had simply disappeared or been disappeared, a fate that tended to happen at airports.

The airport at Managua was crowded and chaotic with people—upper-class people—trying to get flights out of the country. Suor Maria was one of very few trying to get into the country. Suor Maria tried to leave the airport but was stopped. The airport was shut off and all roads were blocked. Maria went around begging and crying and making up stories about needing to get to her community at all cost, to no avail. When that didn't work, she tried Plan B: prayers to St. Joseph. Then she saw a Red Cross van getting ready to pull out. She convinced the driver to take her somewhere, anywhere, in the city. She would fake her way as a nurse, she said. The driver agreed to take her to Archbishop Obando's house, which was being set up as a Red Cross center.

The van had to stop at checkpoint after checkpoint after checkpoint— at least ten or twelve, but they made it. The archbishop received her warmly and entrusted her to some Sisters who were running the center. They sent her to a neighboring house which was being overseen by a young woman while its owners tried to flee to the United States. Despite all the chaos and problems, the Sisters found time to wash, dry, and iron Suor Maria's clothes by the next morning.

She was lucky she had no baggage. Crossing a city that's

sinking into civil war requires a certain nimbleness and flexibility. She wanted to get to the congregation's primary house in Ducuali district, but she was told that the area was surrounded by barricades. She decided to try for the house in Diriamba, 35 miles (60 km) from the center of Managua. The Red Cross gave her a lift to Pochocuape, a poor section of Managua where a Brazilian Sister, Inés Audibert, was trying to run three clinics. She was an angel of a Sister who was not afraid to help and hide people who had been tortured by government forces or wounded in attacks. The Brazilian Sister offered to make the dangerous—perhaps impossible—trip to Diriamba. Suor Maria waved a little white flag out the passenger window as they crept through the worst part of town. They got stopped at a checkpoint, where the Brazilian Sister had to turn back. She left Suor Maria there. Maria kept trying to hitch a ride with the few who were allowed to pass, but no one would stop. Finally a big, black, and very ugly tractor-trailer stopped. The men driving were not Nicaraguans, but she couldn't tell where they were from. They talked in clipped monosyllables. She was pretty sure they were CIA. But they gave her a lift. They took her to the edge of Sandinista territory, where they said they'd have to leave her or they'd be killed. It was about 6:00 in the evening and already getting dark. There was no electricity, no light whatsoever. Some Sandinistas said they couldn't take her up the road, but they could cut through a coffee plantation. They put her on the back of a ratty little motorbike and rode her through a bumpy, slippery terrain of muddy ruts and potholes.

Work in a Troubled World

When the driver could go no farther, he dropped her off. She was almost there, but he told her to watch out for snipers. They were in the trees. She pressed on for another three kilometers. When she finally got to Diriamba, she didn't even recognize the place. All the branches had been sawed off the trees for firewood, and there were barricades everywhere. It looked like a different world. But she found the school building. It was full of refugees and the place was under Red Cross administration. There were people in the classrooms, hallways, stairs, garden, everywhere, everyone with baskets and bundles. Some of the people were from nearby, others strangers from elsewhere. Nobody knew who sided with the Sandinistas, who was sticking with the Somozistas, who was trying to remain neutral. There was a big red cross painted on the roof in hopes of avoiding an air strike, but bombs fell nearby. Each explosion touched off a stampede as people rushed downstairs, dragging screaming children. Sisters were trying to keep people organized, teaching them to share and take turns. The well pump was broken. There were no disinfectants or detergent. The toilets were clogged so people had to use latrines dug in the courtyard. Neighbors, including some of the rich landowners, sent food.

The Sisters spent their nights in desperate prayer. Suor Maria was especially worried about the younger Sisters. If the Somozista soldiers came along, the younger Sisters would suffer the most. Religious convictions would have nothing to do with it. If worse came to worst, the Sisters had a plan to slip out the back and follow a path into the forest. They had their bags packed. They were ready to go.

The overcrowded conditions pushed people to the brink of insanity. The Sisters tried to keep them busy. They formed discussion groups, work parties, games and contests, prayer sessions. People prayed and prayed and prayed. Backsliders converted and promised to change their lives. One woman confessed in public that she was glad her husband had been arrested. He was a drunk who used to beat her. The war, she said, had been good to her. But then the husband escaped from prison and came to get her.

This went on for a month. To fight off boredom, the Sisters played cards, chess, and Chinese checkers. They took turns keeping watch over the refugees, trying to prevent fights and thefts. They took in fugitives who said they needed to hide. They tried to glean news from the radio. Radio Costa Rica could be counted on for truth but never enough of it. Nicaraguan Radio only assured people that calm reigned across the country but that citizens should not go outdoors until the army had finished its "cleansing operation." Reports from various sources conflicted with each other. Some said the Sandinistas were advancing. Others said the government was winning.

From the Italian embassy came an order from Rome: the most elderly Sisters—all octogenarians—were to be evacuated. No one liked this idea, not even the ones who were going to leave the ruins of Managua for the splendors of Rome. It was going to be a major operation to get into town and out to the airport. The ambassador said that if they could get to the embassy, he would get them the rest of the way. So they packed up a Jeep with worries, packages, and a lot of stuff that the Sisters didn't want to leave behind. But they promised Suor Maria they'd be back after the war. As the Jeep growled down a muddy trail, it got stuck every few minutes. Everybody had to get out and stuff branches under the tires to get going again. The older Sisters kept blaming the "communists" for all this trouble.

The embassy was up on a hill with a beautiful view of the whole city, Lake Managua, vast green areas, the volcano that had received the bodies of prisoners, and fires caused by bombings. The ambassador confessed that he did not know how the call for the evacuation had reached him from Rome. He had two teenage daughters who were annoyed because he wouldn't let them go out at night. Classical music was playing loud in the background. When he told Suor Maria that it was to hide the sound of bombs and shooting, she got angry at him, reminded him that those were the sounds of people dying.

The next day two diplomatic cars took them through town. They got stopped at least ten times. Each time the ambassador had to explain who he was, what he was doing, where he was going. But they made it. The ambassador helped them get tickets on the next available Red Cross plane. And then he drove away.

The airport was in chaos, packed with people trying to leave the country. It was dark and without water. The toilets were clogged and filthy. The Sisters spent three days sitting on the floor, depending on people who recognized them to give them food. They prayed as much as they could. One of the Sisters had a huge phosphorescent rosary that shined all night. On the fourth day they got a plane to Guatemala City. The news there was that back in Nicaragua, some Sisters in Sandinista territory had been killed. Everyone cried and celebrated a requiem mass, but later they learned that as soon as the military entered the area, the Sisters fled with a dog and a cat and got away.

Maria returned to the school in Diriamba. There she stayed for the next month and a half until Somoza fled the country, the fighting stopped, and the Sandinistas declared victory. Inexplicably, if not miraculously, champagne appeared and the country began a great party. It involved not only wild celebration but the looting and burning of Somozistas' houses. The looting included just about everything that could be carried out of the MSC school—not just typewriters and desks but doors, windows, and electrical wiring. As life returned to normal, the Sisters started noticing school equipment and a lot of their furniture in the houses of neighbors.

The Somozistas and the upper class fled to Miami, Honduras, El Salvador, Costa Rica, and, in the case of Somoza himself, Paraguay. They also started financing, with the financial and military help of the Reagan administration, the Contra counter-revolutionaries, who operated out of neighboring countries. The Sandinista Revolution blended into another war that would go on for another ten years.

Convinced that the Sandinistas were a communist force that would take aim at the rest of Central America and eventually United States, the Reagan administration established an

Work in a Troubled World

economic blockade of the country. Between the blockade and terrorist attacks by the Contras, Nicaragua suffered many years of hardship. Food was scarce, and many products were difficult if not impossible to find at any price. Visiting Sisters brought the MSCs basic necessities.

Despite the earlier support by religious in Nicaragua, the Vatican and the Sandinistas did not get along. Many congregations left the country, and several foreign priests were thrown out. The MSCs stayed. They reopened their schools, now dedicating them to teaching the poor, who, of course, had no money for tuition. The Sisters asked the Ministry of Education for help, and the ministry agreed under the condition that the Diriamba school teach agriculture because the country was in great need of farms and farm workers. The Sisters agreed as long as they could continue to teach religion. Though in Marxist principle the Sandinistas opposed religion, they agreed to allow religious instruction since the Gospel principles of helping the poor were generally in line with Sandinista policy.

* * *

A certain MSC project had an unusually powerful impact on Suor Maria. It was a physical exertion that became monumentally symbolic. It was just a little school in a little place called Matiguás. At the inspiration of Vatican II, the congregation decided that it had to reach outside the capital. The Sisters felt compelled to go out into the most rural areas where poverty meant extreme deprivation. Such a place was Matiguás. To get there required a 185-mile (300-kilometer) drive down the relatively well paved Pan-American Highway followed by 40 miles (75 kilometers) down a horrendous road that barely qualified to be called a road. Ruts were deep enough to almost tip a car over. Potholes were something a car would drive into with no certainty of climbing out. The holes filled with dirt and dust that turned to mud during the six-month rainy season. Hairpin switchbacks edged along deep chasms. In a memoir she wrote later, Suor Maria called the road a "long khaki snake." The forty miles took no less than three hours. If Maria drove, it took at least four, and a lot longer if the clutch burned out, a wheel rim got banged too hard, or a tire went flat.

The mission was to assume responsibility for a school that was being run by some foreign missionary priests who really wanted to stick to evangelization and catechism rather than broader education. They were also uninterested in Vatican II's call to social service. They'd been out in the boondocks for fifty years. They were exhausted and their standards of hygiene and cleanliness, at home as well as at the school, had, to put it sweetly, slipped. The Sisters had their work cut out for them. Not only did they have to raise standards at the school, but they had to work around the priests, who had little tolerance for any departure from the old way of doing things. They saw no value in improving the community as a whole or elevating the general human conditions. They limited their efforts to spreading the word of Jesus and performing the sacraments—soothing souls, in other words, but not bodies.

The MSC Matiguás mission involved an older Sister as Mother Superior and two younger Sisters. Suor Maria visited from Managua as often as she could.

The Fathers also ran a dispensary but they were a little loose about it. The priest who ran it was very dedicated but not especially well trained in medicine. For example, he confused overweight women with pregnant women. He dispensed medicines, syrups, pills and such with abandon. People were grateful, but they weren't getting what they really needed. The Sisters insisted on letting visiting doctors prescribe medication, but the Father said that if people had just walked 200 kilometers for medication, he couldn't just ask them to come back next Saturday when the doctor was there. The Father wasn't too keen on learning, as evidenced by a tendency to talk for hours at a time without listening to anything anyone else tried to say.

When it wasn't raining, Matiguás was a terribly dusty place, and so was the school. Dust blew in the windows, which were just openings with louvered shutters. Dust also seeped from the hollow-brick walls. The Sisters insisted on having the students spend a few minutes every day cleaning the place. The Sisters also succeeded in planting a garden around their house, providing the town with fruits and vegetables which, inexplicably, people were not able or willing to grow.

Life was tough. The Sisters were attacked by malarial mosquitos, intestinal amoebas, a variety of parasites, and scorpions in the dark. They had to sleep under netting. Until they were able to dig a well, water was often scarce except for whatever rain they could catch off the roof. It was often impossible to find basic supplies, especially during rainy season. The trips to Managua were brutal and uncertain. More than once Suor Maria had to abandon a broken-down car and hitch rides, sometimes in reeking cattle trucks.

As the Sisters tried to bring about change and raise their brother religious up to modern standards, Sandinista activity was increasing in the mountains around the village, and Somoza's military came and went. The tensions lent a political twist to the Sisters' pastoral and liberation work. The Fathers, nervous about the situation, objected to any kind of change. So did the local landowners who knew they would lose land if the Sandinistas ever took over. Most of them considered the Sisters not much more than undercover communists. If change wasn't trouble in itself, it brought trouble.

Still, one large landowner donated a piece of land so that the Sisters could build a new school. The MSC General Superior in Italy arranged funding for the building. But it was hard to get materials and skilled construction workers to come all the way from the capital. Those who came started getting drunk and molesting the local girls. Construction materials had to be watched all the time, day and night, or they would be stolen. Not even the security guards could be trusted, so the Sisters had to watch them. Suor Maria had to accompany the trucks that went to get cement, bricks, and other materials, watch them get loaded, then return with them to make sure nothing disappeared en route. As soon as she arrived, she had to make sure the truck was running right so it wouldn't break down on the next trip, then answer a load of questions about the construction, which was overseen by an engineer who showed up only once. Each day was long, sweaty, and exhausting.

And then it rained and rained and rained. The foundation of the school flooded with water and mud. Workers had to empty it with little cans and cups. Every theft and difficulty cost money. The budget doubled and then tripled. People would no longer accept Nicaraguan currency. It had to be dollars, which had to be bought on the black market. It was illegal, but it was the only way a Sister could get things done.

By the time the school was finished, the Sandinistas had taken power. But then the Contra counter-revolutionaries started attacking anything that seemed Sandinista, that is, anything that was doing anyone any good. The Contras operated out of the same surrounding mountains where the Sandinistas had once hidden. They threatened to burn down the school. The Sisters had to build a wall around it. Then the Sandinista government said that the school should be teaching technical skills, not college-prep courses. But the local people didn't want to learn how to farm. They wanted a diploma that would get them into college so they could get a real job in the city. Students started vandalizing the school. Teachers went on strike and urged students to boycott. When it was time to harvest coffee, everyone—students, teachers, whole families—had to go to a coffee plantation to pick coffee. The Sisters went, too. At one point everyone had to work at night under cover of darkness and in silence because there were Contras in the area.

Every day dozens of wounded and dead soldiers were carried into town. The Sandinistas built a new, if rather small, hospital to replace the old one, which was just a resting place before the grave. One MSC, trained as a nurse, practically ran the place, working day and night to keep it clean and efficient. She developed courses in hygiene and disease prevention. She brought in government and international aid, including doctors and nurses from international organizations. When the dead were brought in, she stayed up all night to patch up their wounds before their families could see them and imagine the pain. She gave herself wholly to help the poor. She went into the mountains to treat people in villages, which gave the Sisters an even more socialistic appearance. She thrived on the constant state of emergency. But Suor Maria saw the Sister losing all objective judgment. She was so dedicated to the poor that she started drifting away from the religious aspect of her vocation. She refused transfer to another place. Eventually she fell in love with a Sandinista commander and left the Congregation. Similar things happened to several younger Sisters. They became more involved with the revolution and the poor than with devotion to God and Gospel. Many ended up abandoning their vocations to follow their own paths toward the salvation of the world.

Despite all the effort at Matiguás, Suor Maria sensed that it might have been in vain. There were isolated cases of success with individuals who, with the help of the MSCs, managed

Work in a Troubled World

to pull themselves up out of the ignorance and poverty. But overall, things were not changing. There was no lasting community improvement. On a long trip back to Managua one day, adrift in reflection, she started wondering whether the mission in Matiguás was really getting anywhere, whether they were making any real progress, whether the school and the community work were sustainable only as long as the Sisters were there to keep it all going. And then she began to grasp something very uncomfortable. She began to think that the Cabrini Sisters were not loved. Here's what she wrote later:

We had been on that mission for almost ten years. We had spared no sacrifices, prayers, ideas, money, initiatives, or people. We faced all kinds of difficulties. We had defended the poor before the deadly attacks of the dictatorship, then defended them from the pressures of the Sandinistas. We even defended them from pastorally oppressive father-teachers, trying to use a new style based on invitation, persuasion, and active participation. We had given the people a real school that was free, clean, and efficient, with programs and real content. We made all our energy, home, and resources available. We had not distinguished between rich and poor even when our tendency was towards the poor, and we had tried to mediate the differences, to heal the broken, to participate in the life of the people without expecting anything. We had gained nothing and, in fact, we had given and almost lost the best Sisters, Sisters who had all paid the price of that experience. We thought that we had loved these headstrong, indifferent, stubborn, difficult people. But why were we not loved?

I could not find an answer. I observed that, despite everything, the missionary Fathers were loved, or so it seemed. Maybe their method was the best, even though for us it was pure sacramentalism. Distribute sacraments, shout, give people what they asked for, do processions in the street, and be left in peace. So, what are we doing wrong?

She talked with the other Sisters about this. They generally agreed. The people simply did not want to change. It was a mindset that had crystalized from centuries of hopelessness, a perpetual situation in which change was always change for the worse. "For whatever reasons," she wrote later, "an oppressed, miserable, meaningless life without a future is preferable to the risk of the slightest change."

In fact, she thought, it was more than a mindset. Matiguás was a symbol of resistance to change, a symbol of a certain reality that exists in the world. The same symbol would apply to a student who failed to learn lessons. If the student wasn't ready, the lesson wasn't going to penetrate. The student would not change. Every teacher knows that, Suor Maria thought. There is a time for change, and there is a time when change cannot happen.

After a few more years, the MSCs decided to pull out of Matiguás. The Fathers didn't want to take the school back, but the MSCs found Sisters of another Congregation—a Congregation with the spirit and values similar to their own—to

Work in a Troubled World

take it on.

* * *

Shortly after the Sandinistas took over, MSC General Superior Regina Casey named Suor Maria regional director for Central America. The times were just as challenging as before. Guatemala, hoping to avoid becoming "another Nicaragua," continued massacring its indigenous population and throwing clerics out of the country. The situation in El Salvador resembled that of Nicaragua under Somoza, with a brutal government battling leftist guerrillas without regard for civilian casualties. The situation in Nicaragua became very difficult. Foreign countries, including the big one to the north, were wary of a regime based on Marxist principles. Imports into Nicaragua were blocked, export opportunities were limited, and foreign investment was virtually nil. The Vatican, under the ardently anti-communist Pope John Paul II, was at odds with clergy in Nicaragua, who were taking the ideas of Vatican II and Medellin perilously close to the gospel according to Marx. The Sandinistas, inexperienced at government, jury-rigged a bureaucracy that depended on the Church for such things as health and education yet resisted support of religion. Attempts at social and economic development tended to get clogged up in incompetent, if not corrupt, ministries. The MSC and other religious congregations saw their people—vocational and lay—leaving just as they were needed the most. Everything was a struggle for everybody, from finding food to getting a flat tire fixed to arranging fuel for cars. People were saying, "We were better off when we were worse off."

Years later, looking back, Maria Barbagallo wrote:

> Life became very difficult, but this helped us to mature and to get closer to the life of the people and to the evangelical sense of the everyday. We Sisters met frequently to look for positive factors in the situation and to try to find a bit of hope for the people. Every family had had one or two people die of grief. We finished our reflections always emphasizing our option for the poor, which was no longer a theoretical matter. If we had left Nicaragua, we would have lost the solidarity with the people who could not leave. Many people, if they managed to rustle up a little money for the trip, left. We were idealistic because we, too, in the long run, were going to show signs of fatigue. Especially irksome, above all, were the endless gatherings that the new government called for the school, the neighborhood, the family, and for the harvest of cotton or coffee. Everyone had to participate in these meetings. The theme of the meetings was always the same: the revolutionary consciousness, the need to remain vigilant, the struggle against the imperialism of the United States. (A North American Sister, very open to ideas, had chosen to come to Nicaragua to work with the poor, but she was disheartened to hear about so much evil in the United States!) When I phoned someplace to talk with a Sister, they always replied: "She's in a meeting."

Work in a Troubled World

Indeed, the same Sisters baptized the meetings as "stupid," and every time I was looking for someone, I was told, "It's a stupid meeting." But the country kept on going, walking between hope, easy optimism, and awful pessimism.

Suor Maria Barbagallo became the vice president of the Conference of the Religious of Nicaragua. It was a perilous position, fraught with a thousand potentials for devastating error. The president, Father Juan Ramon Moreno, S.J. (who was later assassinated in El Salvador), was balanced and serene. He tried to keep the conference out of every possible conflict, of which there were many. There were contingents within the church that opposed the apparent movement toward Marxism and appeasement to the Sandinistas.

One day a handful of people, including a priest and a nun, arrived from Rome. It was unclear who had sent them or with what mission. They asked a lot of questions about how things were going in Nicaragua, what the religious were doing. Suor Maria was open and honest with them. She later heard that they had taken to Rome a rather negative report on the Conference.

In 1983, General Superior Regina Casey came to visit Nicaragua. Between what was suspected in Rome and said in the United States, she had to see what was really happening. Suor Maria saw her as exceptionally serious, but it was hard to guess what she was hearing from Sisters and what she thought about when she heard it. She was accompanied by a cardinal who was telling her that the Sisters were Sandinista sympathizers. He had a tape recording to prove it. He played it, and everyone could hear a Cabrini Sister saying something that was arguably supportive of Sandinista policies. Suor Maria realized that the Church itself had spies among them. The Sisters waited for their General Superior to say something in their defense, but she remained silent and serious. Before she left for Rome, Madre Regina told Suor Maria that she did not like her behavior and that she seemed overworked. Maria said she was disappointed in the lack of support. Regina told her not to take up any more initiatives.

A few months later, Suor Maria received a letter from Madre Regina. It said that Suor Maria was suspended from all her duties as regional director due to exhaustion. She was to be transferred to Buenos Aires immediately. To rest.

She was soon on a flight to Argentina via Bogotá. In Bogotá she met with members of the Confederation of Latin American and Caribbean Religious (CLAR). They all wanted to know what had happened. They'd had big plans for her to represent Nicaragua. She said she didn't understand what was happening, but she wasn't happy about it.

As she wrote in her memoir, "When I found myself alone at the airport in Bogotá with my two suitcases in the middle of winter in South America, after the heat of Nicaragua, I understood that this was an important parenthesis in my life. I neither cried nor despaired nor demanded an explanation from anyone. It was only a matter of choice, one of many in my life: to look forward!"

Suor Maria's Central American experience had lasted just

under ten years. The conflicts, poverty, struggle, and injustice combined well with the resilient community and persistent human decency to reveal that the Christian God is the God of the poor. The culture shock had taught her to be objective, to look in the mirror and see the good and bad in herself. She had freed herself from materialism and taken on poverty. She learned that she was capable of doing something useful and that anything she accomplished could be destroyed in an instant, that she could make the pure, selfless, transcendent choice to be ready to give her life and never see the fruits of her efforts. She learned to face the unattainable mystery of herself and to accept the unbridgeable loneliness that no one can ever reach across. It wasn't the loneliness of being far from family and friends. It was the loneliness that can only be experienced while being surrounded by and deeply involved with other people... yet, ultimately, and emotionally, alone.

Her initial experience in Argentina did little to assuage that loneliness. The Sisters there were cordial but a bit distant, even guarded. They'd been told to expect a very sick Sister from Nicaragua and were surprised to see her walking without crutches. They couldn't understand why she'd been sent there, and they were a bit wary of a Sister coming out of a supposedly communist country. Argentina was in the grip of a right-wing military dictatorship that controlled the media and claimed legitimacy for resisting the evils of communism (though it did not resist launching a war against England over the Falkland Islands). The military government denigrated socialism and anyone who cooperated with it. Not that the Argentinian Sisters distrusted or didn't like Suor Maria, but they apparently weren't sure what to make of her. People in general instinctively recoiled from any language of leftist liberation. The wrong talk could get a person killed. Suor Maria learned to be as careful as she had been in Central America.

After sending Suor Maria to a remote and rustic (and cold) outpost near Córdoba to recover from the trauma of Central America, the Provincial Superior gave her the role of working with young aspirants who wished to enter the religious life. For this she had to travel throughout the country, often with barely enough money to get by. Inflation was raging exponentially, so a trip that cost 100 pesos one way might well cost twice that on the way back. She learned to depend on laity to help her complete congregation assignments.

In 1984 Suor Maria received an unexpected invitation. At General Superior Regina Casey's request, she was asked to attend the General Chapter conference in Rome. MSC leadership from all over the world would be there to discuss strategy and challenges, reflect on their work and their relation to God, and elect a new General Superior. Suor Maria wasn't sure what the invitation meant. Should she be suspicious of being invited to an event and place that might be hostile to Sisters who worked in the leftist liberation of the poor? Or should she be thankful for a gesture of reconciliation from Sister Regina after being unceremoniously yanked out of Central America? She was afraid to ask. In either case, she wasn't going to miss a trip to

Work in a Troubled World

her native land. Baggage fraught with trepidation, she accepted the invitation and flew off to Rome.

The atmosphere at the Chapter was tense and polemic. The big issue was neither liberation theology nor the gospel according to Marx. It was about how the organization was going to survive into the future and to what extent psychology should be applied to the assessment and training of aspirants. The psychological state of the institute was indeed at a point of stress. The average age of Sisters was rising past 65. An institution and its individuals who had once, in the spirit of Mother Cabrini, believed they could do anything were now in despair, believing themselves no longer capable. Sisters saw themselves as too old to have missionary value. Missions were closing. They thought the congregation was quite literally dying.

But this was beyond Suor Maria's control. She was a non-voting invitee, there only to observe. Rather than stand around doing nothing, she asked Sister Regina Casey if she could go to Sicily for a few days to visit family. Sister Regina told her to stay. When it came time to elect a new General Superior to succeed Sister Regina, Suor Maria ensconced herself at the back of the room to work on a crossword puzzle.

But then she heard her name raised. And then again and again, people nominating and voting for her. Caught very much by surprise, she wanted to jump up and withdraw from consideration. She still had time, but she'd have to act fast. It would be easier to withdraw now than resign later. It was very confusing. Was this why Sister Regina had invited her to the

Chapter? Was this why Regina had taken her out of Nicaragua—pulling her to safety before she got into trouble? Suor Maria didn't feel ready for this. It was too much. But as more and more votes were voiced, she began to realize something. She was there for a reason, however unfathomable. If she actually won, she could do more than she had ever done in Central America. She could do so much more for the poor of the entire world.

And then she actually won.

* * *

In 1984 General Superior Maria Barbagallo found herself at the head of a global organization that had served and was serving an important role in a troubled world. But it was an organization with a dubious future. More and more Sisters were beyond the age of retirement, and fewer and fewer young women—potential Sisters—were hearing the vocational call. It was not an impossible situation, but it was certainly a situation that needed to be addressed.

Madre Maria's entire experience with the Missionary Sisters of the Sacred Heart of Jesus had built up to this moment. She had entered the Institute well before Vatican II and begun her vocation in a conservative, traditional convent. She had seen the changes that Vatican II brought to the Congregation and its Sisters, to the Church, and to the world. As these changes unfolded, she had inserted herself into one of the most impoverished and violent regions of the world. She had

Work in a Troubled World

witnessed firsthand the very real battle line between the left and right sides of the Cold War, and she had seen its impact on people. She had made risky decisions based on both reason and faith. And throughout all those years, she had championed a more humanistic approach to discernment, vocation, training, and the option for the poor.

Now she was at the helm of an international organization with issues to resolve and a future to plan.

The first thing Madre Maria had to do was assess the state of the spirit of the Congregation. For that, she set out on an exhausting tour of communities, missions, and projects around the world. As she did so, she realized how much her predecessor, Mother Regina Casey, had dealt with. She had carried forward the renovation of the Congregation in accordance with the reorientation of Vatican II. She had overseen crucial changes to the Congregation's constitution. She had established missionary priorities, above all the theological, spiritual, Biblical, and psychological formation of Sisters. She had overseen the Centenary of the Congregation.

Madre Maria's tour of the missions impressed her with the beauty of the work, the diverse cultures and peoples and the places they lived. The Sisters were beautiful too, sincere in their respect for the church and their love of the faith, of the Sacred Heart of Jesus and Mother Mary. They loved their Congregation and its mission, and they had the highest esteem for Mother Cabrini.

But she detected some subtle but serious issues of concern.

Too many Sisters didn't really understand the breadth of Madre Cabrini's work or the depths of her spirituality. Too many—especially among the oldest—clung to an archaic spiritual mentality of sacrifice and mortification rather than the more mystical spirituality that looked to God's love and the way it can change hearts. Too many feared that the recent constitutional and structural changes seemed designed to shut down missions and projects. Too many felt devalued by the new use of psychology in their formation. And too many had too little hope for the future as they tried to measure apostolic vitality with numbers: numbers of Sisters, number of new vocations, number of missions, all of which were in decline.

These were serious problems, but to Madre Maria, good Cabrini Sister, serious problems are not impossible problems. And they weren't a matter of numbers. They were, to a large extent, a matter of formation of the Sisters themselves. They weren't going to understand the positive changes of Vatican II if they didn't have confidence in themselves and open themselves to the new formation. They had to look to the future, and they had to look back at Saint Francesca Cabrini to understand her and her charism. Too many did not truly understand their patron saint.

Having lived through the difficulties—the impossibilities—of Central America, Madre Maria appreciated and understood the importance of understanding that Cabrinian spirit. So in a crucial decision, she and the 1990 General Council established

Work in a Troubled World

a program of formation focused on the charism and history of the Institute as it revealed the charism of Mother Cabrini—that resilient, persistent confidence and spiritual motivation that let her change with cultural and historic circumstances. During Maria's first six-year term, the Institute organized several international courses. Sisters visited other missions to develop their sense of friendship, confidence, and belonging. They immersed themselves in current theology and charism. They learned things about Mother Cabrini they had never known.

The program worked. Sisters felt a certain renewal, a certain confidence, a certain drive. They redoubled their option for the poor, inserting more Communities in Brazil, Argentina, Central America, Ethiopia, Swaziland, Europe, and the United States. Sisters became more accepting of the various types of missions and Communities. They also accepted a greater degree of independence. But independence necessarily gave rise to more individuality and individual responsibility. Individuality necessarily impacts the cohesion and singularity of fraternity, which, in the case of a congregation of women religious, can impact the common discernment of God's will and prophecy. None of these are mutually exclusive, but Madre Maria feared that the fine line between individual responsibility and fraternal discernment had not achieved an ideal balance.

One symptom of the imbalance was the nationalism she found here and there within the Congregation. She had always worked for an intelligent universalism and internationalism.

Madre Maria also nurtured what may be the most significant development for the future of the Institute—the embracing of Cabrini Lay Missionaries. CLMs became more than auxiliaries to Sisters. They became deeply committed individuals with a sincere desire to grow spiritually and to serve others. Today's CLMs go through a process of formation and discernment as they seek to understand the spirit of Mother Cabrini and the Missionary Sisters who have followed her footsteps into the 21st century. The process ends with a formal commitment to the Institute. As CLMs, they participate in provincial assemblies and even the General Chapter.

Madre Maria's second term as General Superior finished in 1996, but she could hardly be considered "retired." She continued to work to strengthen the Congregation. She had an uneasy concern for its future. Whether the Missionary Sisters of the Sacred Heart of Jesus were many or few, she wanted her Sisters to more fully grasp their charism, their role in the Church and in history. She wanted them to understand that the religious life is not only social work. It is also a prophecy of God's primacy in the world, of God's Word, and of evangelical values. The religious life values sacramental life, accepts the Christian life, and experiences spiritual and material solitude with happiness and hope. It calls for carrying the Cross forward with selfless humility. Madre Maria came to understand all this through the trials and tribulations of her work in a troubled world. Fifty years of it. It was a lot—a big life inside and out.

Argentina

Missions for Dignity and Decency

When Madre Cabrini arrived in Buenos Aires in 1895, it was the largest city in the Southern Hemisphere, and Argentina was one of the wealthiest nations in the world. By 1901, the nation had the tenth largest economy, ahead of Germany and France, and it soon reached the rank of seventh. The economic boom attracted a flood of immigrants from Europe, quintupling the population. But a military coup in 1930 set in motion a steady decline in freedom, economy, and government services. In a few decades, Argentina became a third-rate power under an unceasing strangulation of corruption.

The faltering economy and negligent government made life more difficult for immigrants. Europeans, the majority of them Italians, tended to arrive in poverty. But within a generation they moved from overcrowded communal homes near the port to middle class situations around the center of Buenos Aires. Immigrants from poorer South American countries—Paraguay, Bolivia, Peru—however, had a harder time. They settled into camps on the outskirts of the capital, just hovels of sheet metal and scrap wood on land that no one else wanted. The encampments, known as villas miserables and barrios de emergencia, gradually became permanent neighborhoods centered around a single spigot of running water. Two neighborhoods, known as Villa Amelia and La Salada, took root on a low-lying patch of land between two tidal rivers. The rivers were sluggish open sewers that carried waste into the Rio de la Plata and sometimes, depending on the tides, brought the waste back again. One river ran alongside a municipal garbage dump. When the moon and the tide were right, a single rainstorm could spill a flash flood of fetid, black-gray water into the neighborhood. Sometimes it reached ankles and knees, sometime tabletops, sometimes rooftops. The scrappy little houses were anything but watertight. Floors became mud puddles. It was a vernal cesspool, and people seemed to accept it as their unavoidable due, but somehow better than whatever squalor they had left in the places they used to call home.

The Church showed little concern for these peripheral communities until Vatican II reoriented its efforts. Under the principles of Vatican II, the Church was to "opt for the poor." It would stop serving the interests of the wealthy and instead turn to those who needed physical and spiritual help. Archbishop Monsignor Antonio Caggiano embraced the change

Missions for Dignity and Decency

and devised a program he called the Great Mission of Buenos Aires. It reached across five dioceses, three hundred parishes, comprising some eight million people, 96 percent of them at least nominally Catholic. Under his administration he had as many as 2,500 potential missionaries who had taken vows of obedience. He divided his archdiocese into sectors and assigned each to a Congregation of religious. Then he left it to them to figure out what to do and how to do it.

And not a moment too soon. The world was leaning hard to the left, seething with Marxist outrage, raging with revolution. Marx, it could be said, had opted for the poor a good century before it occurred to the Church. At the same time, the Church was losing its faithful and its influence. Opting for the poor was a perfect strategy for reducing poverty, expanding the flock, and fulfilling the Christian call for mercy, generosity, and solidarity.

Villa Amelia and La Salada were placed under the wing of the Argentine Province of the Missionary Sister of the Sacred Heart of Jesus. The assignment was perfectly appropriate for the congregation founded by Mother Cabrini, saint of immigrants, founder of schools and hospitals. The first Sister to head out to that urban frontier was Madre Virginia Squeri. Born in 1913, she had been with MSC since 1937. She was a teacher at MSC's Santa Rosa school in downtown Buenos Aires. Blessed with exceptional intelligence, energy, and initiative, she was certified to teach mathematics, chemistry, and physics. She played piano. She had a classy, sohisticated air about her. She wouldn't seem to be the sort who would opt to sink her feet into the fetid sludge left by a recent flood, let alone fall in love with such a place, not to mention take city buses for a couple of hours to get there every day after teaching all morning, and then get back on the buses for another two-hour trip back home, arriving well after dark.

In fact, the buses didn't even go all the way to Villa Amelia, no more than a taxi or an ambulance would. The streets were too bad, the crime too violent, the trip just not worth it. Villa Amelia was an untouchable place of untouchables. So Madre Virginia had to walk the last part of the way, invariably weighed down with as many sacks as she could carry. The sacks contained a surprising variety of donated goods—clothes, medicines, cleaning supplies, the odds and ends that somebody always needs. People didn't need to tell her what they needed. She already knew. She knew when a kid needed socks, and she just happened to have a pair. She knew when a family needed a little cash. She knew they would spend it well, and she made sure they actually did. She knew because she knew each and every family, each and every child. She visited each and every home and knew each and every problem. She didn't chat much. She listened. She cared. She told people what to do. And what she told them to do she expected to be done. If it wasn't done, she'd come back. Because she was a mother—everybody's mother.

That's what people who remember her say today. She was my mother. She knew everything, everybody, and what everybody needed. She always cared and she always had a solution. If she caught some father sending his kid out to buy beer, she'd tell

Missions for Dignity and Decency

the father he really should be using his money to fix the roof or put in a floor. And he should be saving some on a regular basis so that someday his family could have a better house. And then she followed up to make sure it was done.

The first thing she told the people of Villa Amelia was that they didn't have to live in the mud like that, that God didn't want them to live that way. Then, like any good mother, she told them that nobody was going to fix the situation for them. They had to do it themselves.

To do things for themselves, they had to get educated. To get educated they needed a school. Villa Amelia had none, and the public schools some distance away were not a priority for the government. They lacked, for example, books, desks, and chalk. It wasn't worth the trip. So in a matter of days—yes, days—Madre Virginia opened a school. As the neighborhood didn't have any real buildings, she gave the first classes under a tree. There she started from scratch. Children didn't know how to read, and neither did their parents. In fact, many people didn't even know Spanish. Many of the Paraguayans were indigenous people who spoke only Guarani. Bolivians and Peruvians spoke Quechua. None of them had books or even a substantive piece of paper. The stub of a pencil would be a family asset shared with neighbors. This was a school starting at the absolute lowest level possible, consisting of little more than heroic intentions, a little shade, and a patch of ground to sit on.

Madre Virginia knew how to put the holy squeeze on people. She got materials for her shady little school, and then she got students from Colegio Santa Rosa to come teach. Then she finagled use of a couple of abandoned train cars that were sitting in weeds not far away. And then a family donated a big piece of land that was adjacent to their house. There she planted a wooden prefab building that would probably rot in no time, but until that time, it was a school. It had three classrooms and an office. And it wasn't just for children. At Virginia's invitation, adults came, too, and not just to learn to read. They learned to sew and then, once Virginia had mastered the craft herself, to fix shoes.

And then she got to work on a bigger building, one with several rooms. It was a school, a workshop, and a community space for meetings, catechism, and other community purposes. It was made of brick, built to last, except that after every flood—three or four or more times a year—it had to be not only cleaned but disinfected. Not an easy task when all the clean water had to come from a single spigot the whole community was using for everything from drinking to flushing.

Madre Virginia came and went every day, somehow teaching a full load of courses in the morning, then leaving straightaway, sometimes without lunch, for Villa Amelia. She stuck her head into homes to see what was happening, kissed babies, berated abusive husbands, checked for infections and malnutrition. She learned new skills so she could teach them to others. Her legs got infected from tromping around in so much toxic mud all day. They never really cured, and she never really stopped to let them.

Missions for Dignity and Decency

And then she got a regular school built. Madre Virginia became a teacher, principal, superintendent, treasurer, personnel manager, food finder, cook, guidance counselor, psychologist, career advisor, and truant officer.

And she kept expanding the school. It soon had classrooms for every grade, from kindergarten to the seventh grade. It had a good solid roof. And it's good it was solid because after one especially deep and sudden flood, she spent two days up there, commanding the recovery from on high. Today the school has a library, a play area under a soaring metal roof, offices for nurses, special education teachers, psychologists, administrators. The government pays the teachers. People donate books. Students pay a little something. The MSCs make sure the school has enough, which isn't always easy. Cleaning and disinfection after a single flood can cost more than an entire year's budget for maintenance.

Seventh grade is about as far as most students can go. After that, they have to make a long trip into Buenos Aires to go to a public school that doesn't offer much or a private school that costs real money. A lucky few get to go to Santa Rosa.

Back then, getting out of Villa Amelia didn't get a kid free of Madre Virginia. She made sure the ones who could get into school actually got into one. She kept in touch after graduation to get them into a profession.

Daniel González knows her from infancy. He was two years old when she came to check on him when his mother was off to work and his slightly older brothers were more or less watching him. When he was old enough for kindergarten, Madre Virginia was there at eight o'clock in the morning to get him out of bed. If he was late, she dragged him off to school the old-fashioned way, by his ear. She was his teacher until the sixth grade. She took him and other kids into the center of Buenos Aires to see the Santa Rosa school, the zoo, museums. She made sure he and other kids went to mass and knew what happened on the Cross and what the Sacred Heart was all about. She got him into high school and made sure he went and made sure he did his homework. She made sure he joined the Grupo Juvenil youth group, which was easy because he loved it. All the kids joined. They went on field trips, played sports, studied the Bible. She taught them, he remembers, about the fundamental essence of life, and she taught them to love it even if life involved standing in two feet of sewage. Right after he graduated from high school, she called him to see what he was going to do next and when and how. Today, he still lives in Villa Amelia. His daughter's doing well in elementary school, and his son is in college, studying accounting. Daniel himself is an electro-neurophysiologist, and he's studying history, too, because he wants to be a teacher. Not bad for a kid brought up in a cesspool.

Mario and Estelle knew Madre Virginia from baptism and on through their years in the Grupo Juvenil. They say she prepared them for life by helping know themselves, by dealing with sexuality, by learning to work, by expanding their vision, by appreciating the importance of a roof. She taught them about consequences, good and bad, things they did. To make sure they

Missions for Dignity and Decency

saw a world outside of Villa Amelia, she organized missions to a place that happened to be called Missiones. It was a remote area up along the northern border with Brazil. It was as poor as Villa Amelia, maybe poorer, but in a completely different way, the way of rural isolation and deprivation.

They arrived at an isolated village outside Missiones via army trucks that Madre Virginia and a local priest had arranged, and they stayed in a kind of warehouse or barn outfitted temporarily with army bunks. The kids were there to help people learn about life in the city, and the people were supposed to help the kids learn how some people lived in a place quite different from an urban slum yet in many ways the same. Both groups were supposed to learn something about dignity even in poverty.

But the lesson turned serious as they figured out that it was a village of slaves. The land all around belonged to a latifundista, a large landowner. He paid his workers with nothing but chits that they could exchange only for food that he provided. People were not free to leave, and they were so ignorant of the world, so isolated from alternatives, that they saw no reason to leave. They brought all their water from a creek. They received no education and not a whole lot to eat. The children were all bitten up by some kind of insect that caused infections and fever and sometimes death. An insecticide could prevent this, but the chits weren't good for that even if there'd been any to buy. The landowner showed no concern.

One day a foreman came into someone's house while Madre

Virginia was there. He had a whip on his belt. He ordered people to stop talking and get back to work. Madre Virginia did not put up with that. She lit into him, yelling that he had no right to barge into someone's house, that those people had dignity and were worthy of respect. She told him to get out... and he did! Madre Virginia and the priest then took the Grupo Juvenil to a nearby radio station and had them broadcast their observations, their tales of slavery, poverty, and disease. People in nearby communities had had no idea of the situation. The landowner's wife found out—she hadn't had any idea either—and soon she had the sick children on their way to a clinic. Then the government intervened. The foreman disappeared and never returned, at least not while Madre Virginia was there.

Madre Virginia did not tolerate any such lack of respect, not from anyone. When the parish priest of Villa Amelia threw a woman out of church because she had separated from her abusive husband, Madre Virginia bawled the priest out, told him that his action was counter to everything that the Church was supposed to stand for, that he had to respect people as people, not judge them for what they did. He asked her to pardon him. She said no, he would have to ask the woman for pardon. Which he did.

Come Christmas time, she told people not to spend all their money on parties and feasts, not until they had a decent roof above their heads, a real floor under their feet. When she held a celebration at a Christmas creche, she went to look for a guy who wasn't there. He was preparing a barbecue for everyone's

Missions for Dignity and Decency

return. In no uncertain words she told him he was celebrating the wrong thing. Jesus, not meat, was the celebration.

Once she blew up at her own Sisters in the MSC house in Buenos Aires. It was during the opening days of the Guerra de las Malvinas, what the English refer to as the War of the Falklands. The war was the perverse brainchild of the president of Argentina, General Leopoldo Galtieri, a dictator responsible for the torture and murder of thousands of alleged subversives. Argentinian media were reporting victories and glorious battles in the Malvinas. His wife, who had been educated at the Colegio Santa Rosa, made a special appeal to the Sisters to pray for Argentina and for victory. General Galtieri himself called them by phone to request the same. One day when Madre Virginia returned from Villa Amelia, utterly exhausted after another long day on aching legs in a fetid place where seventeen-year-old boys were being conscripted into the military, she found the Sisters praying as directed by their murderous president, she exploded with anger. How could they believe that scoundrel of a president and his lies? Did they not know what war was? Could they not see reality? They should not be wasting prayer on the insanity of a delirious dictator.

As soon as she said it, she was shocked at her own vehemence and very sorry that she had brought to her community the pain that she carried in her heart. She rushed outside to the dark of the garden and remained there all night.

Few know how Madre Virginia struggled against feelings of selfishness, sloth, egoism, and impatience. She was terribly sorry for having hurt her Sisters. She berated herself in a book of reflections, called a Memory, that Cabrini Sisters keep, promising to herself and to Jesus that she would be more calm and understanding, that she would avoid arguments and disturbances of the peace. She promised herself that she would never shy away from the truth but also never use it without affection and respect. At other times she warned herself not to expect or ask for any kind of reward for her work, neither heaven nor glory, that she was doing it for the love of Jesus and for His love of the humanity that His Sacred Heart made possible. She wanted nothing more in return for her efforts. She beseeched Mother Cabrini to guide her and give her strength, and she thanked the people of Villa Amelia—the people who knew her as a mother—for teaching her so much about dignity.

Madre Virginia's strength held out for 23 years. Her legs were infected from her first days there, and she never let them rest long enough to get better. They were apparently the source of a weakness that overcame her on August 21, 1991. She was 78.

* * *

Madre Matilde carries a lot of memories. They go back to the little rural town of Pérez in the province of Santa Fe, Argentina, where she was born in 1929 as Teresa Anita Giovagnoli. Her family was of Italian descent and deeply Catholic. The fourth of nine children, she went to public school and worked diligently with the parish. Her devotion to the Sacred Heart of Jesus grew within her. When she was seventeen, a missionary priest came to the village to preach. After hearing young Teresa's confession, the priest suggested that she might be interested in embracing the religious life. Though this idea had never crossed her mind, she didn't have to think much about it. A few months later she enrolled with the Missionaries of the Sacred Heart. With other Argentinian postulants, she did her novitiate in Rio de Janeiro. With much affection and admiration she remembers Madre Elizabeth, a woman of rare intelligence, a polyglot, a Sister of remarkable sweetness and spirituality.

After taking her first vows of poverty, obedience, and chastity in Rio, Hermana Matilde returned to Argentina. She finished her college education and began to dedicate herself to education in the Congregation's high schools. For seventeen years she taught at Santa Rosa in the district of Caballito as teacher and director. Then they sent her inland to Mercedes in the province of San Luiz. There she not only taught but supervised the girls who came from some distance away to study during the week. Sometimes she took them on missionary trips to the outskirts of town. On one of these trips they met a boy who, due to an accident, could not move his legs. Seeing the scant possibility that this boy would ever lead a life of dignity not only for his physical problems but for his poverty and mistreatment at home, Matilde took responsibility for him and did everything possible to help him get ahead. After many operations, the boy gained a certain mobility, was able to study, and managed to get a job at the National Congress, heading the

National Commission on assistance for people with disabilities.

In time, Matilde was named Provincial Superior for Argentina. During her term she made it possible for all Cabrini teachers to receive the monthly retirement benefit they were entitled to as workers in Argentina.

In February of 1979, MSC sent her to Nicaragua to help prepare young sisters for their perpetual vows. It was during the Sandinista uprising and violent government oppression. Like Suor Maria Barbagallo, who was there at the time, Hermana Matilde ended up doing all sorts of things in a deteriorating society. Sandinista guerrillas were becoming bolder. Dictator Anatasio Somoza was becoming more cruel and desperate. Everyone knew what was coming. Hermana Matilde thought she was in Nicaragua just to help new Sisters reflect on God's calling, but she learned that they had a lot more to deal with. They were committed to the people, and many of the Nicaraguan Sisters had families involved in the revolutionary movement. They needed orientation to help them clearly discern what it meant to receive God's call to be a Missionary Sister of the Sacred Heart in the middle of that conflict. At such a time, good judgment in every act was difficult.

The situation was tense when Hermana Matilde and Suor Maria Barbagallo had to fly to Rome for a conference. While they were gone, full insurrection rose up. As Sandinista forces entered the outskirts of Managua, Somoza's National Guard bombed neighborhoods without regard for civilians. Matilde and Maria tried to return, but the Managua airport had been attacked and was under military control. The Sisters had to land in Guatemala. Within a few days Suor Maria was able to get herself smuggled into Nicaragua on a foreign aid plane, but Hermana Matilde and other Sisters couldn't leave until July 19, after Somoza had fallen and the borders were open. They pulled together some food and supplies and drove to Managua and then out to the school in Diriamba. By that time it was empty of the two thousand people who had sought shelter there while it was a Red Cross headquarters. The school was basically intact but essentially a wreck. So Matilde set herself to cleaning it. What else was there to do?

A few days later there was a knock on the door. It was a papal nuncio, there to see how things were going. Matilde told him of their fears, that the future was uncertain, that the MSCs were going to have to make some risky decisions. The nuncio's answer was simple and direct: "You are here to work with the people and for the people. Doing that, what's to fear?"

That was enough of a reminder for Hermana Matilde. She remembered why she was there, and fear had nothing to do with it. After Somoza fell, she and others fully supported programs that raised up all of society. When the new government launched its literacy campaign, she took on classes for children and adults. They used little books that had been published in Cuba—little notebooks that worked quite well. At the same time, the Cuban influence complicated the lives of religious workers. Pope John Paul II's vision of the future wasn't especially encouraging for congregations working with the notably socialist government.

Another major thrust of the Sandinista government was public health and universal vaccination. Hermana Matilde helped with that, too. She accompanied MSC nurses into remote mountain villages to see that everyone got their shots. She remembers one man whom they found eating dirt. They took him to a hospital. After a blood test, a doctor asked, "Is this man dead or alive? He has almost no red blood cells!" The man had been eating dirt in an unwitting attempt to get iron into his body. He was given food, vitamins, and a transfusion, and he survived. But before that was known, Matilde went to his family to tell them that he'd been taken to a hospital. She expected the news to stir a bit of hope, but the family broke down with grief. In their experience during the Somoza years, a hospital was inevitably a step toward the morgue, the funeral home, and the grave. Virtually no one came out of hospitals alive.

Matilde spent three years at the high school in Diriamba, then moved to Matiguás, the remote and very poor village where Suor Maria and others had worked so hard to establish a school and clinic. The work there was constant struggle and hardship. (For more details, see the chapter on Suor Maria Barbagallo.) The local people didn't plant much variety of food, and Managua was too far away for shopping. It was hot and dusty in the summer, wet and musty during the rains. Sometimes the well ran dry. Sometimes rains rendered the roads impassable. People walked miles and lined up in the rain to take classes. Other people stole anything not locked up, nailed down, or watched over.

Missions for Dignity and Decency

In that schools and clinics were part of the Sandinista program, MSC projects in Matiguás were potential targets of the Contra counter-revolutionaries. Matiguás was near Mt. Pancasan, a rugged, inaccessible area where the Sandinista guerrillas once hid. Now the Contras hid there. There were often skirmishes just outside the village. Teenagers used to come to Matilde's classes with assault rifles. They kept them under their chairs in case they were called up to defend the village. Often classes were canceled because so many students were engaged in combat. Sometimes when classes resumed, there was an empty chair.

What the Sisters should do in case of attack was a point of deep reflection. Hermana Matilde, though touched with the courage of her students, said she would take in and shelter her students and the people of the village, but she would never take up arms.

When it came time to pick coffee, a major export product for Nicaragua, the Sandinistas called on every available person to go to a coffee plantation and help. From Matiguás that included every student from the sixth grade on up. Hermana Matilde went, too. Everyone had a bag over their shoulder to hold the little red beans. Many also had a rifle over the other shoulder. The Contras were so near that everyone had to work in complete silence. When Hermana Matilde slipped on a banana peel, she hit the ground without making a sound. At night everyone slept on shelves in a coffee warehouse. Matilde used the few moments of downtime to teach arithmetic and algebra. She wrote numbers and formulas on a wall with chalk.

The visit by Pope St. John Paul II in March of 1983 found the Missionary Sisters of the Sacred Heart, as well as other religious, including priests, at a point of crisis. Although the Sandinistas had put four priests in ministerial positions, the government wanted a clear separation between church and state. It didn't want religion in schools. At the same time, certain priests were stepping outside the ecclesiastical hierarchy by starting "people's churches."

In 1983, when Pope John Paul II gave a homily in Managua, he made a strong call for everyone to remain united with the Church and for priests to be obedient to their bishops. But he made no reference to the hundreds of people who had been killed by the Contras. He didn't mention the many priests and Sisters and other religious who had risked their lives to help people and hide them from the Somozista military. When Daniel Ortega, a leader of the revolution, tried to explain to the pope, at the airport, that his people were in favor of peace and were not against the Church, the pope just read a previously prepared statement, making no reference to Nicaragua's church workers, Sisters and Fathers.

Feeling frustrated, the MSCs returned to their missions. Hermana Matilde, deeply let down, returned to Matiguás well before everyone else. No sooner had she arrived after a painful nine-hour trip than a Sandinista officer told her that the Contras were about to attack. With most of the village people in Managua, there was almost no one to defend the homes. A local commander told Hermana Matilde, two other Sisters, and two pregnant women that they had to leave immediately.

But one of the Sisters said she would not leave. If there was going to be a battle, there were going to be wounded people. She would stay for them. Matilde felt the same. If we must die, she thought, we will die with the people. She set herself to preparing the chapel and other spaces to use as extensions of the clinic. Just outside of town, Contras used loudspeakers to announce their imminent attack, advising everyone to leave. But the defenders stayed. They remained at their posts until 4:30 the next morning. Then Sandinista reinforcements arrived. The Contras never attacked.

After Pope John Paul left, morale among the Sisters was low. They'd gotten used to being unappreciated by the people they helped, but they were hurt to see their pope express no appreciation. In effect all he'd done was warn them and other religious workers and clerics to stick to their religious duties and abandon what he saw as political activities. Provincial Superior Maria Barbagallo called all the Cabrini Sisters together and asked them to write their thoughts, from their heart, on whether the MSCs should stay in Nicaragua or whether it was a waste of unappreciated time. Shortly thereafter, General Superior Regina Casey came to Nicaragua. She spoke with the Sisters. Over the next few months, various Sisters were transferred. Madre Matilde asked for some time to reflect at the community for elder Sisters in San Rafele, Italy.

The Congregation decided to remain in Nicaragua, but

Madre Matilde was transferred to her native Argentina. There she had little time to rest from her grueling years in war-torn Nicaragua. Her new province sent her to the Congregation's Capilla del Monte community near Córdoba, in the foothills of the Andes. Her mission was to support an orphanage there, the Casa del Niño in the nearby town of Unquillo. The Casa del Niño wasn't an MSC operation. Founded and overseen by Padre Hector Aguilera, the organization was a remarkable success. But that success, or rather the assets that made success possible, would become the organization's biggest problem.

When Madre Matilde arrived, the Casa sheltered nearly three hundred children and young adults, many of them with disabilities or who had suffered situations of abandonment, family violence, or social vulnerability. Among them were almost twenty children who were bedridden because they suffered multiple disabilities. The Institute had special teachers, nurses, and doctors. It also gave classes in music, writing, art, and theater. Volunteer mothers provided affection. Young people who could get around kept flower and vegetable gardens that provided a lot of the Casa's food. They also kept a few animals and raised rabbits. They also had a functioning bakery that produced enough bread for the whole place. All of these activities prepared the children so that when they left the home, they would have enough training to find work and support themselves.

Madre Matilde became more and more attached to the Casa del Niño. She could no longer do everything she wanted and

Missions for Dignity and Decency

return to Capilla del Monte each night. She had to dedicate herself to the mission totally, with absolute commitment. That was always her approach to missions. So, with the permission of her superiors, she remained at the Casa.

Mother Matilde's presence visibly improved the quality of life for the children at the Casa. Like any other mother, she cared for one and all. She spent her nights beside the sick, and she was never reluctant to run to the hospital in Córdoba when necessary. The institution was a model of success, evidence that a not-for-profit organization could be administered with solid finances, steady growth, and burgeoning programs that neither business nor government could match.

In 2009, Father Aguilera died while on a trip to Rome. Madre Matilde took over leadership of the board of directors that administered the organization.

On her many trips to the hospital in Córdoba, Madre Matilde came to know a little girl named Belén who was hospitalized there. She was with her mother, a diabetic who was simply incapable of taking care of a little girl in such a fragile state. Every time Hermana Matilde visited the hospital, she stopped in to visit the poor little patient to see if she needed anything. This went on for some time until a doctor told her, quite directly, that they had done everything that could be done for the little girl's physical health, but if she didn't receive loving care, she wasn't going to survive. She didn't want to survive. Hermana Matilde took responsibility for the child and took her to the Casa del Niño along with her mother. The mother would do whatever she could to help out with housekeeping, and she could stay close to her daughter. But the truth was, it was Hermana Matilde who was giving Belén the most affection and attention. It was what God asked of Hermana Matilde: to embrace, as if within the Sacred Heart of Jesus, the soul of everyone who suffered. Today Belén is 28 years old. She has a job, and she works with Matilde, helping to sustain her as she approaches her nineties.

One of Hermana Matilde's most outstanding accomplishments was securing disability pensions for every patient in the Casa. She spent every day over the course of years to make sure each person got his or her due and, above all, the medical attention to which they were entitled.

Meanwhile, the political and business environment of Argentina was boding ill for the orphanage. The political situation deteriorated into corruption and uncontrolled favoritism. The Casa del Niño had several properties that it had received as donations. One was a house where children could take a little vacation beside a stream in the mountains. But these properties, worth millions of dollars, became of interest to real estate developers. The assets of the Casa del Niño became a liability as the government lay its corrupt hand on it. Under the influence of businessmen, the provincial government began to strangle the organization. It prohibited certain people, including many employees, from going to any of the houses. Government financial support was reduced to the point where the buildings could not be maintained or even cleaned. Government contributions of food were limited.

Missions for Dignity and Decency

Employees were paid so little that qualified people would not work there, and each person who remained had to do the work of a person and a half. The remaining children, who were the most chronically ill or disabled, suffered from incompetent dispensing of medications. Medication is often complicated, involving syringes and intravenous delivery—not something for amateurs or volunteers. Eighty-eight years old, Madre Matilde had to go running around to courts and attorneys, trying to secure the care that the children are entitled to.

When she wasn't running around trying to make the legal system work, Madre Matilde was with the children. When she visited, the children, normally dull-eyed with boredom, came to life. Their eyes opened and they smiled in their individual ways. The ones who couldn't talk made cooing sounds. Madre Matilde had a kiss and a hug for everyone. She told them that they were beautiful. One fifteen-year-old, his limbs twisted and deformed since birth, confined to bed, fed by tubes, slept almost constantly. His life depended entirely on the correct doses of medications and food fed into his stomach by tube. He was in the care of women who were no more trained than maids. But when the boy heard the sound of Madre Matilde's voice, he awoke. When she stroked his face and kissed his cheek, his eyes beamed with delight.

In its continuing efforts to disable the organization and make its properties available to developers, the provincial government also replaced the Casa's board of directors. Despite the previous board's exemplary work over the previous forty years, the new board showed minimal interest in making the organization work right. But the Casa was still functioning, so the government prohibited many of the employees from entering the property. That included Mother Matilde, but she simply disobeyed, just as any other mother would. She could not let her children go without her care.

Then many of the children were sent to other institutions, and some were returned to the families who hadn't been able to care for them in the first place. In some cases these were situations of extreme poverty. In other, neglect or even violence and abuse. Most of the children who were left at the Casa were those who had so many physical problems that no one else was willing to take care of them.

In 2015, creeks in the area overflowed in heavy rain. Many houses were flooded. Inside the Casa del Niño buildings, the water was three feet deep. Madre Matilda was horrified since more than fifty children were either in wheel chairs or confined to bed. The water left living conditions worse than ever, and the houses began to stink. The oven at the bakery was ruined. Soaked with muddy, polluted water, the houses became moldy and in worsening disrepair. For a while, the entire maintenance budget went into cleaning supplies and disinfectants.

Madre Matilde stayed with the Casa del Niño for as long as she was physically able. Even as she approached the age of ninety, she was driven by her missionary zeal and remained firm in her commitment to the love of the Heart of Christ. She always followed that Cabrinian motto, from Philippians 4:13—

"I can do all things through Christ who strengthens me." And by 2016, when she retired, she had done all she could.

Central America and Mexico

Standing with the Poor

Zona 6 in Guatemala City is a *zona roja*—a red zone. It is controlled by criminal gangs. If there's any security, it lasts for only a couple of minutes when a delivery truck drives in and a guy in a bullet-proof vest with a pistol-grip shotgun slung around his neck gets out to stand guard. Then he gets back in the truck and leaves. The streets belong to the gangs, not the government. Though the gangs are generally referred to as narcos, narcotics themselves are only one of the criminal pursuits. The preferred criminal activity is extortion. They go to each home and each business and demand weekly payments, under threat of death. For the sake of credibility, the gangs always carry out their threats. When people run out of money, they have no choice but to flee town or even leave the country. Territorial gunfights break out in the streets. People get hit.

There's no ambulance, not even a taxi to an ambulance, not even a three-wheeled *tuc-tuc* motorized rickshaw to a taxi. Zona 6 is an island in a city of deeply troubled waters.

Were it not for the crime, some families in Zona 6 might manage to live at the bottom fringe of the middle class. According to the Missionary Sisters of the Sacred Heart who know them, they are generally good people and hard workers. But even with a good heart and hard work, many live deep in permanent poverty. Many are in shaky, ramshackle shacks that cling to a steep incline above a murky river of sewage. Their sidewalks are steep, rough-hewn concrete stairs. Waste water from these little homes flows down PVC pipes to the river. After a thunderstorm, when the water is high, people go down to the river to toss away their garbage. It won't take much of an earthquake to send the whole slum down into the river. Not far away is an even more precarious settlement. It doesn't need an earthquake to send it sliding into the river. A heavy rain will do. It's just a matter of time.

Several MSCs and lay workers run a small clinic in Zona 6. It's called Dispensário San José. The Sisters live within walking distance on a stark but quiet street ending at a dusty park with benches and soccer fields. Dispensário San José is about the only establishment in the neighborhood bigger than a tienda off somebody's living room. Everything else has been extorted out of business.

Hermana Maria Concepción Vallecillo has worked at the Dispensário four times since the 1980s. She first went there when she was 23. It was her first mission as a Cabrini Sister. She was just out of medical school in Managua. As a young girl, she'd witnessed the revolution in Nicaragua, and she saw it worsen as she got older. She did her medical school internship in makeshift combat hospitals. It wasn't just on-the-job training. It was extreme religious work toward a degree in social medicine—medicine with a social purpose, a purpose other than money. She embraced social medicine, religious work, and liberation theology all together as a single pursuit.

After the war, Hermana Concepción continued in social medicine. She had seen a lot of young lives lost, and there was still much to do as the brave, new nation struggled to rebuild itself. In time, Concepción burned out and had to stop for a while. In 1989, she agreed to go to Guatemala, where civil resistance was degenerating into genocide. At the time, Zona 6 was poor but still relatively safe. The Dispensário San José was just a dilapidated house of questionable wood. It was serving about three people a day, but over the next several months, as Hermana Concepción applied her skills and experience, the dispensário was treating some sixty patients a day.

She remembers an eighty-year-old man who came in with asthma. He was desperate for air but had only one quetzal, less than a dollar. The price of air—which is to say, the price of asthma medication—was three quetzales. Hermana Concepción dropped the price to one. The old man could not accept such generosity. He said he'd come back with the other two quetzales. And he did. It was dignity, Herman Concepción says now. The people had dignity.

At the time, between the civil war and a corrupt and negligent government, people outside the capital were suffering terribly. The military often massacred entire villages, claiming that its people were communists. At the same time, guerrilla fighters demanded food from villages. As a result, people were malnourished and sick. Most doctors refused to leave the safety and comfort of Guatemala City. In 1989-90, Hermana Concepción and others visited the especially impoverished departamento of Quiche. She remembers finding herself in a village with no children. She asked where they were. A woman told her they had all died. Nobody knew what they'd died of or what to do about it. It was probably measles, which was killing children across Guatemala. But the government was unconcerned about anything so distant from the capital.

In 1992 Hermana Concepción worked with CONAVIGUA, the Coordinadora Nacional de Viudas de Guatemala, the National Coordinator of Widows, widows of men who had disappeared—or, more correctly, been disappeared—in the war. She worked with a Carmelite Sister and four Basque atheists. The widows had little hope of finding out the fate of their husbands, let alone being able to do anything about it. Under a murderous government, the best they might hope for was their own survival. They were risking their lives for people who had already died. But they had to look for the ones they loved. Hermana Concepción saw something in them. It was the grace of God. These simple peasant women taught this worldly

Sister something about grace and the reality of Central America. From them she learned a new way of religious life.

Later that year she transferred to Bárcena, a town on the outskirts of Guatemala City, on pastoral mission. In 1993, she was sent to Managua again. In 1995 she was sent to Spain to study theology. In 1999 she returned to Guatemala. The next year, Sister Lina Colombini, General Superior, visited the Dispenário San José and recognized the need for improvements. She found funds for a new brick building on the same site. Concepción and other Sisters reorganized the clinic. It now offered not just emergency medical treatment but odontology, gynecology, ultrasound, EKGs, and a clinical laboratory.

One of the new programs was called Promotores de Salud Mental—Promoters of Mental Health. By 2004, the program grew to include 54 trained women who monitored their friends and neighbors for signs of domestic abuse, depression, addiction, and related problems. It was a very social idea, using the community itself to root out widespread but hidden mental health issues. These neighborhood outreach monitors were the only way for the dispensário to see into the secret side of Guatemalan society, the inside of homes where men ruled with an iron fist and women assumed subservience. People accepted this as a way of life, and they kept quiet about it. No one was trying to stop it or even deal with it. Certainly not the police or Guatemalan social services. The program at the dispensário included support groups to deal with the effects of poverty, violence, and oppression. Not that anyone could put an end to such entrenched problems, but at least a few people could better understand how to survive the ongoing traumas.

By that time Zona 6 was already changing for the worse. The government had negotiated an end to the fighting with the guerrillas. Part of the agreement was that the government would offer cobertura, which could be translated as coverage, referring to a general government policy of providing human services—healthcare, education, security—to the whole population, not just the minuscule upper class. But once the guerrillas had turned in their weapons, the government forgot about its promise. Services and conditions grew worse and worse. The drug trade moved into the vacuum left by a failing economy and dysfunctional government.

In 2005, Hermana Concepción transferred to New York City to study English and learn more about medicine. She worked with Sisters Diane Olmstead and Pietrina Racuglia to help immigrants, many of them refugees from Central America. She was at the other end of the pipeline of migration that began in Central America and flowed north. It was a pipeline of people, fear, and desperation, a pipeline out of a frying pan and into a fire. America was a land of opportunity, but the streets sure weren't paved with gold. The struggles of other lands became different struggles in a different world. Madre Cabrini had dealt with this same phenomenon more than a century earlier. The MSCs were still dealing with it. From Central Asia to Central America, the causes of migration were as bad as ever, in some ways worse.

Standing with the Poor

In 2015, Hermana Concepción realized something about her work. She was visiting the Mother Cabrini Sanctuary in Chicago. It was a place of prayer, worship, devotion, pilgrimage, evangelization and reconciliation. It was right there that St. Frances Xavier Cabrini had once worked in the socio-economic turmoil of burgeoning 19th century industry and immigration. But Concepción found the place just too calm and under control. It would seem to be a nice place for a nun, but it was uncomfortable for a Cabrini Sister. She felt closer to the spirit of Madre Cabrini back in Guatemala City, working with people who needed help.

And to the Dispensário San José she returned, now for the fourth time, arriving in 2016. She found Zona 6 radically worse than the way she'd left it. The narco gangs had almost total control over the whole area. Extortionists were making it virtually impossible to survive there. They had so much power and caused such fear that they no longer had to go to individual homes and businesses to demand payoffs. They could simply go to one resident and demand that he collect tribute from everyone in his neighborhood. If he didn't, he would be killed. Not might be killed. Would be killed. Killings were happening two or three times a day. No one was exempt, not even sidewalk vendors trying to earn a pittance off nothing more than candy displayed on a cardboard box.

Extortionists went to a school and demanded that the administration collect and hand over 40 quetzales for each student enrolled. Or else. The administrators couldn't accept

113

that, so they closed the school. Now the school operates like an underground organization. Teachers distribute lessons and learning materials secretly. The locations and dates of exams are shared in guarded whispers.

Extortionists also forced the closing of a dispensário run by Jesuits. The Jesuits told patients they would have to use the Dispensário San José, which was oddly, inexplicably, and perhaps only temporarily, exempt from attempted extortion. The Sisters suspect it was because they had once treated someone involved in the gangs, someone powerful enough to demand respect for the Sisters. The Sisters had apparently given love to someone who needed help, and now it seemed to be coming back to them. They don't know what they'll do if the extortionists come. Trust in God? Risk their patients? Risk themselves? The Dispensário San José is about the last social service in the zone. The government's gone. The police are gone. The Missionary Sisters of the Sacred Heart are about all that's left.

Also inexplicable is a steep decrease in usage of the Dispenário San José. It offers a broad array of services not available anywhere around there. The dispensário is more than the word dispensary might imply. It doesn't just dispense. It's an outpatient clinic with doctor, nurse, dentist, psychologist, and laboratory for an array of tests. There's a Niño Sano—Healthy Child—program. There's pre-natal care and chronic care. There are psychological services for everyone from children to the elderly. Every Monday there's a program for senior citizens. On Tuesdays there's a program for children under the age of five.

Standing with the Poor

On Wednesdays, school-age children can join in educational and social activities—everything from field trips to computer training. Thursdays are for pregnant women, many of whom are barely halfway through their teens and whose pregnancy was anything but voluntary. Fridays are dedicated to chronic care. Zona 6 needs all of these services. Public hospitals are not only negligent but hard to get to from a place with little public transportation. Public schools don't offer much besides chaos, certainly no extra-curricular activities. Nobody has any money to spare. Violence is rife not only in the streets but in homes. Yet usage of the Dispensário San José has declined by half since 2008. Why?

Hermana Concepción is trying to answer that question, to diagnose the problem. The Dispensário San José used to be the safe place in Zona 6. Now, though people need a safe place more than ever, too many stay away. The dispensário seems divorced from the community. People want help—need help—but they don't ask for it. They don't support it as a community. The lack of support leaves the place more vulnerable to extortionists. With funds and personnel scarce, if the community does not use the dispensário, it will have to close.

After a few weeks of preliminary analysis, Hermana Concepción came up with a vague but observable diagnosis: social depression. Like a severely depressed person, the community has lost its strength, its energy, its will, and all sense of self-worth. It has fallen into total, absolute despair. Bereft of hope, it has given up trying to help itself. People have withdrawn into themselves. They are no longer a community. In that humans are social by nature, a lack of community can only lead to social problems, a spiral downward into self-perpetuating problems.

So the work of the Sisters in Zona 6 must necessarily reach beyond standard clinic services. To promote health, it has to promote community, and to do that, it has to somehow reconstruct the social web—the interconnectedness, the interrelationships, the interdependence.

Among the MSCs working on this social web are Hermana Norma Beatriz Caal Lopez and Cabrini Lay Missionary Angelica Perez Rivera. Hermana Beatriz has been with the Missionary Sisters for the last 20 years, serving in Nicaragua, Argentina, Rome, and Mexico. Now she is the coordinator of the Dispensário San José. She knits together a staggering variety of services and programs—medical professionals, pharmacists, technicians, staff, medications, supplies, volunteers, educational materials, patients, and participants young and old. In the maelstrom of violence, poverty, and self-imposed social isolation, in one of the worst parts of a city that is barely above anarchy in a country that is proving to be all but ungovernable, she is trying to educate the community in the many simple ways that people could improve their lives. They need to know, for example, that a doctor, not friends, should tell them which medications they need. They need to see a doctor before they feel sick. They need to treat their children like people, not pests. It all adds up to more than a full-time job...and it's not all she does. She also works with parish youth as they struggle to survive and grow up under difficult and often dangerous conditions.

Angelica, a Cabrini Lay Misssionary, has been with the MSCs in one way or another since 1975. She was on track to become a Sister, but when her mother fell ill, Angelica, the only daughter, had to care for her. She now runs the Programa de Adultos Mayor (PAM), the Senior Adult Program. The dispensário adopted the title *Adultos Mayores* because it seems nicer than terms that imply elderliness or a late stage of life. *Mayor* can mean greater, bigger, elder, senior, higher. The program is far more than a senior center. These people, being over the age of 60, are dealing with the same problems as the rest of the impoverished population. But their share of the problems is raised by the exponent of old age. They're more likely to need medical help, less able to earn money, more often isolated or left without support, more often malnourished, more poorly housed, and suffering more pain. Virtually none of them gets all the medications they need. They rely on reduced dosages and home remedies. In sum, they suffer more stress just as they are less able to deal with it. Under such circumstances, psychological problems—stress, depression, and worse—are inevitable.

Angelica has about sixty adultos mayores active in the program. They meet at the Dispensário San José every Monday, and fifteen of them meet at the El Rosario chapel every Friday. Much of the purpose is subtle psychological support. For some, it's a weekly opportunity to talk with others who have some notion of what it's like to be getting old in a place that challenges human tolerance. But it's also a chance to just plain have fun. They dance. They do tai chi. They have parties. They eat well. They celebrate Mother's Day, Mother Cabrini Day, Christmas, Easter, and any festival or religious day that serves as a good excuse for a party. They hold raffles. They go on field trips. They visit the sick. They take care of their own and others. Just as life might otherwise seem bleak, they feel valued and purposeful. Satisfied. Happy to be alive and looking forward to next Monday.

The MSCs run another dispensário, the Dispensário Madre Cabrini, in the Barcena area of Villa Nueva, a suburb contiguous to Guatemala City. It's a tough neighborhood. The extortion isn't as widespread as in Zona 6, but domestic violence is rife. Domestic murders in Barcena can reach two or three a week. Irmã Laudir Crócoli, a Brazilian who has served in rural Brazil and Paraguay, explains that wives in Guatemala are essentially owned by their husbands. They are kept in line through the forces of not just violence but economics and ignorance. Women generally have no control over household finances. If they want a coin for a Coke, they need to ask for it. If a husband wants to spend the rent money on beer, there's nothing his wife can do about it. Wives never have much of a profession and thus remain economically dependent. They don't even have much of an education. They are educated only enough to serve as wives and mothers. Cultural values force them to keep household problems a secret. They suffer every kind of abuse without telling anyone.

Standing with the Poor

Irmã Laudir works with Hermana Xochilt Calero to help some fifty *adultos mayores* stay healthy and sane. They use an approach that cares for health, spirituality, and psychology. The group meets every Tuesday to play games, reflect on the Bible, exercise, dance, and talk about their experiences. What they talk about most is hunger, abuse of children, and how they themselves were abused—psychologically if not physically—when they were children. Generally speaking, the hunger gets worse with age, and the anguish of child abuse never goes away. People need to talk about it even decades later. So the Sisters listen to what's being said and what's not being said. They try to figure out what needs to be done, whether it's to come up with some food or medication or call a priest or fill the hole of loneliness. If someone doesn't show up to meetings, someone goes to check up on them. If someone needs psychological counseling, they get it, even if they are in their last days on earth.

Culture and tradition also result in child abuse, either malicious or aggressive abuse or simply mistreatment that is considered normal. Sexual abuse is common, and it is not unusual for adolescent girls to be forcibly impregnated at home. Thus begins their life of de facto slavery. In general, children are ignored and demeaned, "educated" with low-level violence such as ear-pulling and spanking. They're often left filthy from either lack of care or lack of water in the house. Poverty often leaves them malnourished and suffering from the usual consequences of hunger.

An ordinary clinic would treat nothing more than the symptoms of these problems. The Dispensário Madre Cabrini is trying to treat the root of them. One especially innovative and effective initiative, a joint program with Caritas International, is Madres Monitoras. It's a lot like the Promotoras de Salud Mental but aimed at young mothers and their small children. Volunteer mothers keep an eye on new mothers in their neighborhoods. Oddly enough—and this is an indicator of the breakdown of community—people in urban neighborhoods barely know each other evenm though they are close neighbors. Everybody keeps to themselves. But the Madres Monitoras open doors. They find out who's pregnant, who just had a baby, and how the babies are doing. They weigh and measure infants, keep records, and track their growth. They get women talking to each other. They suggest solutions to problems. With the help of Caritas, the Dispensário Madre Cabrini distributes vitamins and foods where needed. In late 2016, over fifty monitors were overseeing some two hundred children in eleven neighborhoods. In these neighborhoods, the monitors know all the children and all the women who have or soon will have a child.

But food alone doesn't solve the problem. Women need to be enlightened and informed. They need to know that they must, and can, take control of their lives, that they can be leaders in their communities. Through programs at the dispensário they learn to achieve a certain level of independence by starting their own nanobusinesses—anything from sewing to food preparation. They learn that clean children and clean kitchens result in less illness and thus less money spent on medical care. They learn how to bathe children with nothing more than soap and a bucket of water. They learn that children become better adults if raised with love, kind words, encouragement, and affection.

One thing young women need to learn is when to have children. Not that they always have much of a choice. Some of the mothers are just fourteen. One in five babies is born to a teenager. Needless to say, few are planned and many are outside of marriage. Fathers have a tendency to run off and leave the mother to take care of "the problem." Young girls end up living with their mothers, who may be still young enough to be having babies. Being a Catholic organization, the Dispensário Madre Cabrini prefers not to engage in direct pregnancy prevention programs, but they help girls grow into stable, assertive, self-sustaining women. That emotional and economic stability helps them become mothers—and better mothers—when they feel it's time. The same applies to teaching boys to grow up and then become responsible fathers.

Birth control wouldn't solve this problem at the root. The more productive, healthier, pro-life solution is to give young people something to do, to nurture their self-esteem, to give them hope for the future. They need the kind of "life projects" that get them working on education, self-improvement, job training, and career planning.

This process of human improvement starts well before the advent of puberty. A children's program called CHISPA starts forming better people when they're not much more than three feet tall. Twelve volunteers give kids an educational environment not found in public schools. It's an environment of support and motivation. The capacity, potential, and limitations of each one are considered. A lot of the kids show up suffering the consequences of malnutrition and problems at home. One boy, for example, wasn't able to grasp a pencil. Now he's an artist. One shy girl shrank into a corner. Now she's a leader. The program introduces kids to computers and English. It nurtures their creativity with crafts, drama, art, and writing. They learn the magic of saving money by making deposits into little banks. When it's time for a party, they plan it themselves. They learn that they can make things happen.

Making things happen. What could be more Cabrini?

Hermana Maria Elena Plata, coordinator of the Dispensário Madre Cabrini and director of MSC operations in Guatemala, knows how to make things happen. Under her guidance the dispensário has grown to include a doctor, a dentist, a psychiatrist, a gynecologist, an ophthalmologist, a physiotherapist. The dispensário can do ultrasounds and X-rays. It can do tests for everything from diabetes to zika. Consequently, the Dispensário Madre Cabrini is highly respected—so much so that people are asking the Congregation to expand it into a hospital. As it is, people would rather go to the dispensário than to the public hospital, which is anything but respected. The most common request is for obstetrics—a decent place to have a baby.

Hermana Maria Elena doesn't think the dispensário can

become a full-services hospital, but it has the potential to become a kind of super-clinic. It could treat injuries, deliver babies, offer short-term care. It could expand its services into the community, that is, to the causes of symptoms that send people to a hospital. There's just one problem—the usual problem: money. A rather substantial amount would have to come from outside the Congregation.

Not that she needs something else to fill her idle hours. She works ten hours a day on weekdays. On Saturdays, she works with parish youth. She dedicates one Sunday each month to an Orientación de la Vida—life orientation—program for adolescents. Another Sunday is for youth leaders from eleven communities. Just one Sunday per month is for rest. Because once in a while everyone, even Cabrini Sisters, need to rest.

* * *

Juanita Zoraida Mendoza Sandino was born in 1945 to a Nicaraguan family she describes as politically committed. Dinner table conversations often included political discussions. Her brother was a communist opposed to Nicaragua's dictatorial government. This was back in the 1950s, two decades before the rebellion really rose up. But the Sandinistas already existed as scattered resistance. Some of them used to meet in little Juanita's house.

She remembers a time when she was nine years old. She saw little girls her own age selling tortillas on the street. She asked her mother why. Her mother said it was because they didn't go to school. A while later, Juanita was doing some homework under a mango tree in front of her house. A little girl came along and asked to see her book. She didn't know what it was. The little girl held it upside down as she pawed through the pages of unintelligible black squiggles. Juanita asked her, with some surprise, whether she knew how to read. She didn't. She couldn't go to school because she had to watch her seven brothers and sisters while her mother made tortillas to sell. So Juanita ripped a page from the book and started showing the girl the letters and how they formed words. She started with the letter O. A while later, a little shoe-shine boy came along. He wanted to learn to read, too. So Juanita started teaching them. And there she was at the age of nine, teaching at a school under a mango tree.

And then her brother came along and recognized the nobility of what they were doing. He said no, a school can't be outdoors on the ground. He had them all come into the house, where they set up a classroom. He rustled up some paper, and they got to work.

As Juanita grew older, the situation in Nicaragua—the struggles, the poverty—called her to support changes that were necessary. She thought change was urgent if future generations were to live in a different kind of country. But she didn't know what to do. Her interests were in teaching, theology, pastoral youth activities, and theater. She knew she was supposed to be interested in getting married and starting a family, like everybody else. She had plenty of friends and boyfriends, and little by little all her friends got married and went down the family trail. But she was reluctant to follow them. She didn't know why and didn't know what to do.

She talked with her priest. He told her to drop everything—university, friends, theater, everything—and go away to discern for seven days. She went to the house of a friend outside the city. She prayed intensely, asking for the help of the Spirit of God. She walked in the woods. She thought. And she came to understand that her life was not for family. That world was too small for her. She wanted to work for a much wider world of people, and she trusted that God would show her how.

In her pastoral youth work at the national level, she came to know 35 Congregations that worked with youth groups. It was the Missionary Sisters of the Sacred Heart that grabbed her attention. They worked with the poor. They went all over the world. They did what she wanted to do. She decided to accept their invitation to experience the missionary life. She accompanied them on missions to help the poor, and she learned about Santa Francesca Javier Cabrini and her life of intrepid dedication. After a few mission experiences, Juanita went to her mother, by then a widow, and told her what she'd like to do. Her mother started crying—but not because of the common parental perception of losing a child to a convent. No, her tears were of a certain joy. With the birth of her nine children, she had offered each to a saint. When Juanita was born, her mother offered her to the Sacred Heart of Jesus.

Before Hermana Juanita took her first vows, the Missionary Sisters of the Sacred Heart assigned her to the Colegio La Inmaculada in Managua. It was right across the street from the Universidad Centroamericana. Juanita wasn't too happy about the mission. It was too easy, too cushy. As a postulant she'd already worked in marginal places on the outskirts of Managua: Loma Linda, Torres Molina, Pochocuape, and San Isidro—impoverished places that were beyond the government's ability to improve. She asked why the Congregation couldn't have a community in places like that. People there, she knew from experience, were very enterprising. They just needed some support. The answer from above was that she was too young and too new to religious life. So she appealed to a higher authority. She asked some of the older sisters to pray for her plan. She didn't tell them about her intention to establish some kind of house in one of those rough neighborhoods. She kept that between herself and God.

In November of 1972, she took her final vows and assumed her position at the Colegio Inmaculada. In December, an earthquake destroyed the Colegio along with the rest of Managua. All the Cabrini Sisters withdrew to the school in Diriamba, normally 45 minutes away by car.

The Superior General, Sister Regina Casey, came from Rome in profound solidarity to see how the Institute of the Missionaries of the Sacred Heart of Jesus for Nicaragua could collaborate. It was decided that the sisters who had previously been working in those marginal places should return there to

Standing with the Poor

support people however they could. These neighborhoods had not suffered the earthquake maybe because they had already been earthquaked, so to speak, throughout their lives by the poverty and abandonment they suffered. Their houses were of cardboard, sheet metal, and scrap wood. The sisters participated in several meetings convened by the Conference of Religious of Nicaragua to suggest criteria for assistance and how religious organizations should channel the international aid that was coming from many countries.

The Somoza government sent the Army to distribute aid that had been donated by other countries, but aid was being distributed according to the government's political criteria. Aid was only for people known to support Somoza's political party. This caused some tension with the army, but the MSCs and the people they were trying to help told the army that the sisters were going to do as they had planned and that the donations from other countries did not belong to the government. Distribution was to be made according to the needs of families. The army had no choice but to accept the proposal, and the sisters dedicated themselves to distributing humanitarian aid.

And it was then that the MSC Regional Council of Central America accepted the initial proposal to build a small house in Loma Linda to serve the poor areas where the Sisters had already worked. Hermana Juanita thought, "God takes a while, but does not forget." Her cry had been heard, and God had manifested his desire in that decision. Juanita was very happy. It was the second Regional MSC community in a slum.

Loma Linda means "Pretty Knoll," but it wasn't so pretty. It was a place of bars, brothels, poverty, violence and filth. But it was wealthy with rubble, and with God's help, it was possible to build a little house from the debris of the Immaculate College. And from that humble beginning grew the Instituto Tecnico La Inmaculada. A dirty, dangerous, forgotten part of town today has a school where young people study a technical career. With a baccalaureate diploma they can work, help their families and continue studying. The Instituto Tecnico La Inmaculada is one of the most respected schools in the city.

For the next 45 years, Hermana Juanita moved through nine countries, learning from every culture she experienced. She worked in Chicago, New Orleans, Philadelphia, New York, Mexico, Italy, Guatemala. She was especially drawn to that most Cabrinian mission of working with migrants. But at the same time, she was always working for social and economic justice, the mission she'd been on since starting her school under the mango tree. In 2007, in cooperation with the Scalabriano fathers, she helped to establish the Centro de Latino Americanos in Rome. In that same year, she, along with Hermanas Carmen Pantano and Beatriz Caal, was in the first group of sisters who organized a house for migrants in the harsh, violent desert town of Altar, Mexico, just south of the U.S. border.

Most recently Hermana Juanita has been working in Guatemala City, living in the community in Zona 6. She works at the Dispensário San José but has also taken on a struggle for justice near a precious metals mine called Puya. It's not far outside Guatemala City. Like mines all over Latin America, it manages to evade the law, contaminating streams and creating veritable cesspools of water toxic with the rejects from the mine. Puya's mess includes a toxic pond and a stream that is eight percent arsenic—still drinkable if you want to take your chances, but if it gets any worse, it will be nothing but a stream of poison. Around the mine, wells have gone dry. Kids have developed skin problems. After being caught committing numerous crimes too egregious to ignore, the mining company was told to suspend operations, though it remained unpunished and not definitively shut down. Apparently activity has more or less ceased, but people hear helicopters fly in and out at night. Nothing is being done about the toxic pond, which is likely to overflow during heavy rain. Despite a constitutional requirement, the Guatemalan government has failed to order the mine shut down and cleaned up. The issue has gone to Guatemala's Supreme Court, but the court has declined to take action.

To get the government to adhere to its constitutional mandate, people from the Puya area have set up camps near the mine and also outside the environmental protection agency office in Guatemala City. Outside the environmental protection office there's a big tent in between the edge of a busy highway and the government building. They call the encampment *Puyita*, Little Puya. People have a right to be there, but only if the camp is constantly occupied. If it's unoccupied for a minute, the government can shut it down.

Constant occupation of the two camps is a burden. While the people at Puyita put up with the constant roar of traffic and the threat of collision (which has already happened once, miraculously without injury), people near the mine, just outside of town, are living in tents. They are dependent on water and food being trucked in. They cook on wood fires, and resort to an outhouse. It isn't a pleasant place to live, but toxic ponds and streams aren't pleasant, either.

This has been going on for over four years. The protesters aren't getting much sympathy, let alone assistance, but Hermana Juanita goes to visit them. She brings them moral support in the form of prayer, love, and the implicit support of the Church and God. She reinforces what they already know—that they are locked in an important struggle. It isn't just Puya it's all over the world—simple people defending land and life against aggression by big corporations and governmental negligence. Hermana Juanita brings the Puya resisters the message that they are involved in something far bigger than themselves, that they aren't alone, and that God, too, is with them.

When Hermanas Juanita, Beatriz, and Carmen went north to establish a safe house for migrants in Altar, Mexico, the new mission was a shift for the Congregation. Or, more accurately, a reorientation. MSCs had come to the realization that, though Madre Cabrini had been dedicated to helping migrants, the Congregation she established, about to celebrate 125 years of missions, didn't have a mission in Central America dedicated to migrants. The Congregation decided that a big party was not the Cabrinian way to commemorate the founding of their organization. It would be far more appropriate to open a mission to help migrants. Central America and Mexico looked like the place to do so. Honduras and El Salvador were suffering the same onslaught of drugs and crime as Guatemala. Life was increasingly intolerable. Innumerable families under the screws of extortion faced the choice of being killed or fleeing. The logical direction to flee was north. Mexicans weren't much better off. People headed north not with visions of gold-paved streets but with the simple, human desire to live without fear. But they had no idea of the difficulties and dangers of the trip. So the Congregation set about discerning where help was most needed and would be most effective. The decision required a lot of research and thought. Should they establish a mission in a country that the migrants were fleeing? Or at the southern border of Mexico, where the real danger began? Or were they more needed toward the end of the migration, near the U.S. border or even on the other side of it? What were other organizations doing? Where was the need most desperate?

Migrant journeys from Central America, across Mexico and then over the border are never less than excruciating. Sometimes whole families, or fragments of families, set off with little or no money, quite possibly without documents. Some are single mothers with babies. Some are pregnant. Some are kids. Some have "coyotes"—some honest, some not—who show them the way or take them part way in a van. Some have no idea where they are going or what to expect. What little they carry is almost always stolen before they get far into Mexico. Often as not it's the federal police who do the stealing. Starting in southern Mexico, people often ride atop northbound trains, clinging to tankers and boxcars in rain and sun, depending on people to throw them food. It's a long, slow, dangerous trip fraught with every risk, from rape to murder. For good reason these trains are known as The Beasts. In Mexico City, various Beasts go north toward the States. One Beast crosses the Sonora Desert before slowing down near the town of Altar. People jump off here. It's as close as they can get to the border, which is still about 60 miles (90 km) away.

At one point, ten thousand people were drifting into Altar every day. The town was a stopping point in a pipeline of human catastrophe. People arrived in utter destitution and desperation only to find that the town was totally controlled by drug and human traffickers. These so-called narcos feed off the world's poorest and most vulnerable people, people with no money, no friends, no alternatives, no information, no plans, no place to stay, nothing to eat.

They also have no way forward, no way back. No migrant leaves Altar without paying tribute to the narcos. The price is a thousand dollars or more, which is good for a trip up to the border. Sometimes the attempt to get to the border leads the migrant into a kidnapping. Families back in Central America have to come up with thousands of dollars just to free their loved ones—who still have to come up with money to get to the border. If they can't, well, there's an alternative: haul 60

Standing with the Poor

pounds of drugs across the border in a backpack. There's also an option to sell an organ or two—a kidney, a cornea, some blood—at a clandestine clinic in Altar, but that doesn't really pay enough to get a person out of the situation.

Hermanas Juana and Concepción visited all eleven borders between Guatemala, Mexico, and the United States, looking for the place where life was most threatened. After a year of research, they presented their findings to the other Sisters of the Region. The Sisters agreed that Altar, being one of the worst places in the world and a focal point of desperate migrants, was the place to go. The mission was given to Hermanas Juana, Carmen, and Beatriz. Six months later, when Juana became regional director, Hermana Mercedes, a Guatemalan sister in temporary vows, joined them.

They arrived in 2009 to find a gritty desert town surrounded by a stereotypical desert of cactus, mesquite, thorns, sand, dust, rattlesnakes, and stark sierras thrusting up through the heat waves. Here summer temperatures exceed 120°F (50° C). Winter temperatures dip near freezing. The town is under strict control of the merciless narco-mafia. Only the parish priest is allowed to witness the consequences of innumerable murders. Only he is allowed to drive up to the border without asking permission. He can give last rites over bodies of migrants found out in the desert, where they have to remain unburied. He knows the houses where kidnap victims are held. He is allowed to know such things and witness such things because it is understood that he will not go to the police or report to

133

an outside organization. If he tried to do anything about what he saw, he'd be dead, and the people in town wouldn't have a single individual who could cross from one world to the other. And, as odd as it sounds, even the narco-mafiosos want to have a priest in town,

But to say that narcos control the town is not to say that everyone is a narco. Quite to the contrary, most people are good-hearted and doing what they can to survive and stand up for the good. The narcos don't bother them too much. The victims are the migrants. The Sisters arrived in town to find a volunteer organization already offering help to migrants. It had started as a Bible group that collected food. Then the parish built a house where a few migrants could stay for a day or two as they recovered from their trip and prepared for the ten-day trek across the desert. The house had a couple of dormitories stacked with bunkbeds, a couple of storage rooms, a couple of bathrooms, and a kitchen big enough for no more than a family. But what it needed most was someone to take full-time charge of the operation. It was a big job.

It was also a new kind of job. The Sisters had to work with an existing organization of volunteers whom they very much needed. Not only that, but it was a unique place (to say the least) with a unique community laced together by mysterious ties and relationships that make it possible for such a town to survive and remain civil. The Sisters couldn't just walk in and take charge, making their own decisions. They had to consult and cooperate with the volunteers, which is lovely, of course, and certainly better than working alone, but also it's stressful—a layer of assistance but also a layer of concern.

The house, known as the Centro Comunitário de Atención al Migrante e Necesitado (CCAMYN) (Community Center for the Migrant and Needy) is on an unpaved street a few blocks from the center of town. Its sign is faded and covered with the pale dust of the street. Steel grates guard the windows. The door looks like it never opens, but it does if you know how to turn the key, yank the knob and give it a little kick. It opens into a dining room with a long table that can seat some forty or so people. At the far end, a full-wall mural depicts the hellish journey from the south with images of trains, a truck packed with bodies, a skull on the ground, crosses in the desert, Nuestra Señora de Guadalupe—the patron saint of death and suffering—blessing peasants. The kitchen barely fits four people. The dormitories are out back, across a hardscrabble courtyard.

Migrants can spend three nights in the dormitory and can come eat for up to five days. The occasional exception might be made for people in serious medical condition. Every morning migrants gather at a side door. If they haven't been there before, one of the Sisters or a volunteer interviews them. They need to know names, ages, religions, where they're coming from, where they hope to go, the basics of what they've suffered along the way. The stories are heart-rending. Everyone arrives traumatized. In fact, they were probably traumatized before they left home. That's why they left. Everyone has been robbed. Some are unaccompanied children. Some are just infants with their mothers. Some of the women are pregnant. Most of the women have been raped. Almost everyone has seen a fellow traveler die. Of every ten who cross into Mexico, only six make it to Altar. Some who arrive are trying to cross the border for the second or tenth or fifteenth time. Some have returned from an attempted crossing during which they were injured, beaten, robbed, or raped. Some have just arrived in town and have no idea of the dangers they face. But they know they are hungry, and they know that sleeping outdoors wouldn't be a good idea, and by word of mouth they know that there's a place they can spend a few nights and get a bite to eat.

Today CCAMYN is run by Hermana Marta Nidia Lanzas Navarrete, who arrived in 2012, and Hermana Ana Gilma Argueta Cifuentes, who arrived in 2014.

Hermana Marta knew about the MSCs from an early age, when Sisters first visited Loma Linda on the outskirts of Managua. The Sisters hadn't even established a community yet, let alone the school they would eventually build there. She was impressed that Sisters had come from far away to help the poor people in her neighborhood. She wasn't sure about becoming a Sister herself, but she signed on as a Cabrini lay missionerary, the first in Central America. In 1991 she was assigned to Guatemala, and by 1994, she knew what she wanted to do. She became a novice and was sent to Argentina for three years. There she had the privilege of working with Hermana Virginia in Santa Amelia. Then she went back to Nicaragua to teach at the school that had risen in Loma Linda. She also taught at the school in Diriamba, where she was director of the primary school. Then she was off to Madrid for spiritual formation. A year later, she took her perpetual vows. She then accepted a mission in Nicaragua and Guatemala. In 2012 she took on the challenge of Altar.

Hermana Ana Gilma knew from about the age of eight that maybe she wanted to become a nun. She was afraid to tell anyone except a blind woman who lived next door. For some reason she could only tell someone who couldn't see her face. She was growing up in Zona 6 in Guatemala City when some Italian priests invited her to a retreat. There she took on a stronger sense of vocation and missionary urge. But still…she kind of wanted to get married, too. But she saw more satisfaction in loving God than loving a man, more freedom in religious service than in marriage. She got to know several Congregations. It was the missionary life of the Cabrini Congregation that appealed to her most. She wanted to join them, but she was way behind in her schooling. She hadn't finished primary school until she was fifteen because she was the oldest of four children in her family. When her two young brothers got old enough for school, she had to drop out. The family could afford only so much education. So the MSCs took her under their wing while she finished high school in Managua.

Formation had her going back and forth between the two countries. Maybe God was watching over her. She was in Guatemala City in 1972 when an earthquake destroyed Managua. She was in Managua in 1976 when the big earthquake destroyed Guatemala City.

She earned a degree in teaching. For the next thirty years she would be either a teacher or a school director. In 2013 she visited Altar, just to have a look. She saw the place and sensed a certain need there. A certain calling. Later that year, on sabbatical in Italy, she told Regional Director Gilda Mercedes Mendoza that if a position opened up at Altar, she'd be willing to serve there. And with that, Hermana Ana Gilma, sixty years old, started a new career. She was no longer a teacher. She was attending to some of the world's most desperate and downcast people.

Altar was completely different from anything either Sister had ever seen or done. Hermana Marta remembers wondering how life would be in such a place. She was nervous about the mission but not quite scared of it. She had a great desire to work with people in such desperate straits. She didn't know that the numbers of them would be in the thousands in a town ill prepared for them. Sometimes CCAMYN feeds eighty to a hundred people per day, though the number goes up and down with seasons and economic conditions. Sometimes it's more Mexicans, sometimes more Central Americans. The people who come through and the conditions that drive them could serve as a meter of the human condition, the problems of Latin America. (Other migrant routes could measure the human condition of the whole world. While Altar was receiving a lot of Central Americans, other towns were seeing people from Asia, Africa and South America tending to follow their compatriots.)

Standing with the Poor

Feeding dozens or scores of people every day is expensive and arduous. An American organization, No Más Muertes (No More Deaths) sends food—rice, beans, coffee, cans of soup and "Mexican-style" diced tomatoes. Local families donate chicken and tortillas. A supermarket donates 1,500 pesos (about US$75) each month. During busy times, the Sisters have to come up with thirty or forty kilos of beans each week. When they have enough money, they buy items such as toothbrushes, backpacks, first aid kits, the kinds of things the migrants need for their long hike across the desert.

So at dawn each day, either Hermana Marta or Hermana Ana Gilma (they take turns, one of them staying home for prayer and reflection) and a couple of volunteers cook up a concoction of whatever's on hand and serve it with sweet coffee. Once the plates are laid out on the table, their migrant guests troop in. Some have spent the night in the dormitory; some have been waiting at the door. The Sisters offer a Christian prayer, and if there are non-Christians present, they offer a moment of silence for their prayers. Then they sit. There is little talk, just the sound of forks scraping every crumb, grain and bean from plastic dishes. They bring their plates to the kitchen window and slide them across the counter. Each and every one of them says in humble tones, "Gracias, Madre."

The Sisters do what they can to prepare the migrants for the last and most dangerous part of their journey. They warn them about unscrupulous coyote guides. Some coyotes will walk migrants around the desert for 10 days, then point to distant lights and say, "That's Phoenix. Buena suerte, amigo. Good luck. Except the lights turn out to be Altar. Others will lead the migrants and their backpacks of marijuana across the border, then kill them. Some get bitten by snakes or stung by scorpions. Some break ankles and are left to die. Women are inevitably raped. The Sisters give the migrants pamphlets explaining how much water they have to carry, how to look for flags that Americans have left to mark stashes of water, how to get unlost by looking for lights, cell towers, highways. They give them used clothes and shoes donated by local people. They give them the warm, loving words that people need so they know that despite their unspeakable travails—God loves them and so do some people.

Migrant guests are allowed in early in the morning and late afternoon. The Sisters are brusque in their instructions. Rules must be obeyed. No exceptions. Before a migrant steps in the door, a Sister wants to know where they're coming from, how long they've been in town, how they heard about CCAMYN, who around there, if anyone, they know. The instructions seem stern because the operation has little room for deviance. It's on the edge of too many problems, from money to emotions to violence. One thing the Sisters are sniffing for is undercover coyotes. They try to sneak in, maybe just for a free meal, maybe to try to recruit clients, maybe to lure people into a kidnapping. The Sisters can smell trouble. They live in a sea of it.

They or a volunteer conducts more detailed interviews in a little office. The vitals get noted in a book. One reason is to establish a record of who has come through. Many of these people will disappear in the desert. When families come looking for information, at least they will know that the missing made it as far as Altar.

The Sisters are also listening to—caring about—stories of suffering, cruelty, desperation, abuses, horrors that no one would share except maybe to a Sister, a surrogate mother who can love without judgment. This is the hardest part of the mission. Every story is an emotional burden, and the burdens weigh heavily. For a while Hermana Marta had to stop taking the incoming interviews. It was too much for her. Hermana Ana Gilma says that part of their job is to control their own emotions. They don't become callous to the pain they witness, but they have to know how to deal with it, how to keep it at a distance so they can help without breaking down, without crying.

They heard, for example, the story of the young Guatemalan man who headed north with his brother. At the border of Mexico, a gang attempted to kidnap them. The brother got killed. The other had to flee. He had to leave his brother's body behind. Going home was not an option. He had to keep going north, for his family. He felt his brother's death was all his fault. The guilt was killing him. He wanted to die.

They heard the story of a young woman from Chiapas. She was trying to join her husband in the United States. She headed into the desert with a group of other migrants. Far from anywhere, she broke her ankle. The rule in such situations—and they are many—is cruel yet understandable. The group can't stop, and nobody, after all they've been through, is going to stay behind. So they left her there. With torturous difficulty she managed to hobble to a highway. She returned to Altar. The Sisters nursed her for a year until she could walk. Then she set out again. That time, she made it.

They heard the story of a young man who was kidnapped. He was sodomized before they let him go. He was physically and mentally traumatized. The Sisters let him stay until he had recovered physical and mental strength. Then he set out again.

They heard the story of a young man from Honduras, a civil engineer with a college degree. The gangs there make everybody pay a "war tax." They tried to extort his aunt, who sold fruit at a sidewalk booth. She couldn't pay it, so they killed her. They also killed her two sons. As the family was leaving the wake, someone fired a machine gun at them. They had to flee. They couldn't even go home. He, his almost blind mother, a cousin and her 18-month-old baby all headed north with no money and no documents. They were atop a train when the federal police of Mexico forced them off. But his mother fell off the other side of the train. He followed her, and they ran. He has no idea what happened to the rest of his family. At some point he became separated from his mother, too. When he arrived at CCAMYN, he slept for days without waking up and without eating. The Sisters could barely arouse him. Later, he said he found a place to stay, but he still comes in for food. He doesn't know what to do but try to cross the border.

But wait a minute...Hermana Ana Gilma says his story

doesn't add up. There's something strange about it. She was actually able to find his mother by calling safe houses to the south, and she got the mother on the phone. But the mother said she didn't want to talk to her son! She was finished with him. She never wanted to see him again.

So Ana Gilma has her eye on him a little more than she has her eye on everybody. It's that kind of a town, that kind of a mission. You need to know who you're talking to. You need to know the rules. The Sisters are relatively safe as long as they don't get in the way of the narcos' money. Helping a kidnap victim escape could be a deadly effort. Once the parish priest confided to Hermana Mercedes, just a new sister at the time, that he knew of eleven migrants from CCAMYN being held in a house. With astonishing boldness and confidence, Mercedes went there and talked to the guy at the door. He said there was no one inside. But another guy came along and said there were indeed people being held. Somehow Mercedes talked them into releasing the people. Soon 21 people came out. One of the narcos asked her for a certain quantity of money because he had just fed all those people. It wasn't fair that they were all leaving without paying a ransom. Hermana Mercedes pulled all the money from her pocket, which was just loose change, and said that was all she had. She'd come back with more. But the Padre told her not to bother. So she didn't. And somehow the incident went no further.

The MSC mission at Altar has little room for error or rest. A mistake can cost lives, even threaten the viability of the whole mission. The work is almost constant, if not serving up food for twenty or a hundred people, it's finding the food to feed them, cleaning up, washing sheets, taking in, sorting, and distributing clothes, coordinating volunteers, hearing stories of human horror, offering solace and prayer. The Sisters do what they can for people for a few days. Then the people head north and are never heard from again.

* * *

Hermana Gilda Mendoza was born in Guatemala, the oldest of three daughters. Her family was of modest means but wealthy in love and faith. Gilda knew the MSCs from their first days in the country in 1969. The Sisters often came to Gilda's mother for assistance as they put down roots in Guatemala City. Gilda often helped them, and by the time she turned fifteen, she knew she wanted to join their Congregation. When she told her father, he refused to allow it until she finished high school. She dutifully did so, all the while spending more and more time in the Sisters' new house in Zona 6. She often worked late and had to spend the night. She was practically living the life of a Sister before she asked to become a postulant in 1973. The Sisters agreed to let her do a preliminary "experience," and her father agreed. On the day before Christmas Eve, she boarded a van bound for Nicaragua. It was a hard time of the year to leave a family behind. When the van pulled away, she looked back. She saw her father crying.

Standing with the Poor

She soon arrived at a community of 17 Sisters of various nationalities in the town of Diriamba. There she worked with Hermana Albina, from Spain. Sister Albina had worked with Madre Cabrini, and she loved to call Gilda to come sit with her and hear her read about the saint aloud.

She was assigned to Escuela Sagrada Familia in Managua to work on catechism and work with Sister Lucrecia in ecclesiastical base communities. By July Gilda was accepted as a postulant. Early the next year, 1975, she was sent to the novitiate in Guatemala for formation. Under the direction of Regional Superior Maria Barbagallo, she studied with young women from Argentina, Spain, Italy, Nicaragua and Guatemala. She saw Suor Maria as a model of rectitude, openness, love, and activism, a Sister with a passion for the institute and its history. The novitiate was international and intercongregational. Part of the program involved sending three Sisters from as many Congregations into the rural areas of Guatemala to work on catechism. Most often these were small, impoverished communities of indigenous people. Working with a translator, they participated in Gospel reflection groups. The experience inspired a deep change within Sister Gilda. These simple people in remote villages were so deep and sensitive in their faith and devotion. Their religious lives were a lesson for the young Sister from the capital city.

Hermana Gilda took her first vows in 1977. In 1980 she returned to the school in Diriamba. In 1985 she took her final vows. This was in the years following the revolution as

Nicaragua pulled itself up from the decades of destruction and dictatorship. The "Contra" counter-revolutionaries made this difficult process all but impossible. The government insisted that the school adopt a more practical program of technical agricultural education. The conversion was quite compatible with the Institute's opting for the poor. But the change in orientation brought allegations of the Institute shifting to Sandinismo and socialism/communism. There was contention within the Church, and people in religious life working for the poorest of the poor were considered Sandinistas. It was during these politically and economically stressful years that Hermana Gilda became sub-director and then, in 1994, director of the school.

In 1995, the Conference of Religious of Guatemala put out a call for human shields—people to serve the purpose of standing between men with guns and people who feared getting shot. In this case, the people were Guatemalans who had fled to Mexico during the horrific bloodshed of the civil war. The violence had not ended completely, but some 1,200 people were ready to come back to their country, if not to their native villages. They were allowed to come settle in a place called Nuevo Futuro in Ixcán.

The Missionary Sisters of the Sacred Heart heard the call. Helping migrants was well within their mission, no matter how dangerous. Sister Gilda and Sister Barbara Staley said they would go. If someone wanted to shoot the returning refugees, they'd have to shoot a couple of MSCs (and other volunteers) first. Organizers assigned them to a ranch, which they shared with a young American and a priest.

As it turned out, the need was for more than human shields. The refugees had to literally build a new village made from the earth where they stood and the forest around them. There was some international assistance, but ultimately it all depended on a group of simple peasants. It was a very precarious situation, impossible were it not for the human spirit and faith in God. To Sister Gilda, it was a life-transforming experience. She witnessed the miracle of community, organization, and cooperation as everyone worked for the common good. Every day she and Sister Barbara had to accept a meal from a different family. The people had so little, yet they always had something to share.

The Sisters didn't just stand around not getting shot. They participated in night watches. They comforted families. They shared in celebrations of the Gospel and the Eucharist. They went down to the river to help women with laundry and to serve as shields. They could see soldiers on the other side of the river. They heard army helicopters overhead.

Years later Sister Gilda wrote, "This experience made me aware of the suffering of my people. It was a great human and spiritual growth. I learned that it is important to not do too many things and to not believe myself a hero. What is important is to be there to listen, to walk beside others, to be able to give and to receive. I thank my Congregation for this opportunity to discover the signs of the times in the historical moment our people live in."

In 1997, she became Regional Superior, the first of two terms. The next decade and a half would become increasingly difficult for the school in Diriamba. The government cut back on its financial support. By 2008, the school was no longer sustainable. To Hermana Gilda's deep dismay, the school she had loved since 1973 had to close. The Institute still owns the building, but it is rented to the state for use as a university and occasionally other levels of education.

These were also years when the Missionary Sisters of the Sacred Heart began to work with Cabrini Lay Missionaries (CLMs)—men and women committed to the Cabrini charism but without taking the vows of a Sister. It is these lay people who make two Cabrini schools in Managua—the Instituto Técnico Inmaculada and the Escuela Sagrada Familia.

The Escuela Sagrada Familia, which is alongside the MSCs' house in the Ducualí part of Managua, operates under the Cabrini charism. The school teaches pre-school through the sixth grade, a total of about six hundred children. About forty percent of them are from poor families, many of them exempt from tuition payments. The Ministry of Education rates the school as "excellent," which is better than it can say about its own schools, where administrators often don't even care how their schools are rated. Families have been asking to have Sagrada Familia expanded into a high school—not only for the academics of it but because when sixth-graders graduate and go to a public high school, they are traumatized by the lack of discipline and the low level of the classes.

The Instituto Técnico La Inmaculada is the same school that the Missionary Sisters of the Sacred Heart founded in 1974 in Pochocuape, a district on the outskirts of Managua just after the 1972 earthquake. Today the school is a beacon of hope in the gloom of persistent poverty. For many years, the school was a bunch of bare-bones buildings of galvanized steel that became dangerously hot under the sun. When General Superior Sister Lina Colombini came to visit, she saw the need for something better. Steel ovens are not a good learning environment. She found the money, and today the school is a quadrant of concrete classrooms around a courtyard as lush with nature as a tropical park. Mango trees offer not only fruit but shade. Every once in a while a palm drops a coconut. Ferns and flowers grow along paths. Birds chirp. But the little park isn't there for just shade, fruit, and birdsong. It's a subtle lesson in the importance and beauty of nature, which is an important part of the school's overall curriculum.

The classrooms here are a bit overcrowded with as many as sixty students in a room, but conditions are far better than in public schools, where there may be seventy students in a class. In fact, though the Instituto is in one of Managua's poorest areas of Managua, it is considered one of the best schools in the country. All of its graduates hold certificates in marketable technical skills such as accountancy, computers, gastronomy, or languages, and eighty percent of them go on to higher education. It's proof that poor kids can do as well as rich kids if given the chance.

The Instituto Tecnico La Inmaculada, also known informally as the Escuela Hermana Lina Colombini, is under the direction of Hermana Emperatriz Canales Espinosa, who is also a Regional Counselor. She has taken to heart the relatively recent Cabrini strategy of working with lay missionaries, and they have taken to heart the charism that makes Cabrini schools work so well. They have a vocation for their work, and some of them have been with the MSCs for decades.

One teacher describes the school as "a mission rich in love." Another says, "Here we are forming the people who will change the world." Another emphasizes the holistic education that brings together academics, technical skills, spiritual health, and Christian values. Another points out that the school reaches into not just the minds but the hearts of students. It develops their human side, the side all but ignored in public schools. Education transcends students, families, and community. Students have to be engaged in the community, and families have to be engaged in the schools. Students are taught to not just do but to do good and do it well.

In 2016, the school had 1,154 students spanning pre-school to high school. Though tuition is low, it's a real burden for some families. Parents often work second jobs just to keep their children in a school where they are safe and each child receives attention. Government support has diminished. Where it used to pay all teachers, now it pays for just 13 of the 66. The school depends largely on outside sources for financial support. With careful management of funds, the beyond-the-call-of-duty attitude of teachers and lay missionaries, the school hopes to reduce the size of classes. The school is always trying to improve, always asking families what it can do better.

More funds could certainly be put to good use. A water well would be nice because the neighborhood often has no public water. Classrooms still have steel roofs, and temperatures inside can reach toward 100°F (38°C). Kids get dehydrated and pass out in class. The gym needs a new roof. The computers need upgrading. The library needs books and shelves. If they had some chess sets, they could start a chess club.

The lay missionary teachers and directors like to work here. They know that they are doing something good. The "profit" of this private school—its motivation—isn't money but love. It promotes solidarity among students, families, teachers, and staff. They all work together for the common good and common values.

That difference could be summed up by the Cabrini charism, the one Madre Cabrini brought to Nicaragua in 1891. She got expelled from the country before she got much done, but her Sisters came back in 1921. And despite a century of political and geological upheaval, they are still here, and so is Madre Cabrini's charism. And every day that charism is sown like seeds in the minds of young students, the people who are going to change the world.

Brazil

Churches of People, Churches of Brick

Maria Eliane Azevedo da Silva was born in a town in the Brazilian state of Minas Gerais. Since she was little she dreamed about helping people. She remembers the time a missionary priest came to her town and spoke at the church. The townspeople took in his words and felt comforted by them. Little Maria Eliane wanted to have the same impact on people. She remembers taking up a garden hose and speaking into it as if it were a microphone. She imagined people listening attentively, and she imagined that her words were touching the hearts of everyone so that they might live better.

Ever since she was a child she liked to play at being a teacher. By the age of fourteen, she began to teach. She gave private lessons to adolescents who were a year behind her in school. It was a big step up from talking into a garden hose. And that's when a prescient priest asked her if she had ever thought of opting for a religious life. She hadn't. In fact, she'd never even seen a nun. But the question remained in her head like a little seed. So one day when she was reading a newspaper published by the diocese, she felt herself attracted to a list of books. One of them was about Mother Teresa of Calcutta. She ordered a copy and read it. She was entranced by the life of an Albanian Sister dedicating her life to the poor in Calcutta. Little by little the desire to be a Sister grew. She mentioned it to her parents, but they didn't support the idea. But when she was old enough, they sent her to Rio de Janeiro to continue her high school studies. They were hoping she would forget her desire to be a nun. Her godmother said that if she studied at a Catholic school for a while, she might change her mind. But something else happened. Eliane began to see from close up how the life of the nuns at the school was, and her desire to become a Sister grew. As a student she began an intellectual and written development of her thoughts during that time.

She became a real teacher impassioned by the mission of education, and at the age of twenty she began her professional career at the Catholic school where she had studied. When she was 21, she was looking for a boardinghouse in Rio de Janeiro where she could live. That's how she came to know of the Congregation of the Irmãs Missionárias do Sagrado Coração de Jesus. This boardinghouse was at the convent beside the

Churches of People, Churches of Brick

Regina Coeli High School in Rio. The property had been bought by Madre Cabrini in 1908, when she came to Brazil. There Eliane received as a gift the book Viagens de Madre Cabrini (The Travels of Mother Cabrini). She fell in love with the contemplative, mystical life of Madre Cabrini. She loved the saint's capacity to persist in doing good and accomplishing so much during her lifetime.

The little seed the priest had planted in her head finally sprouted and flourished. When she was 22, she decided to enter the religious life. Her wish to help people matured, and her innovative capacity was notable when she worked at a nursery school in São Paulo. The school needed an outdoor area under a roof where children could play. She got parents and teachers to work togther to construct an such an area.

The experience—or rather, the success of the experience—taught her something. She saw that she had transcended her own capacity. She'd done the kind of thing that Mother Cabrini had said could be done.

After that, Irmã Eliane's life was a whirlwind of educating others and herself. She took her perpetual vows at Regina Coeli High School in Rio Pomba, did pastoral work in local villages, and soon became director of the school. She returned to São Paulo to serve as Provincial Secretary. At the same time, she took a Master's degree in the Sciences of Religion. She wrote a chapter for a compendium of religion sciences. She did post-graduate work in psychology. She volunteered at the Center

155

for the Migrant. In 2011, she became Provincial Superior and began revising the strategic plan for the Province and its schools. She wrote articles for educational magazines.. She also wrote a book: *Eduque a Si Mesmo e Seja Feliz (Educate Yourself and Be Happy).*
Brazil is not an easy place to get things done. New legislation often makes things more difficult. The economy is in recession, the federal government is in chaos, politicians are corrupt, and there's little funding to support the social work of religious organizations. Irmã Eliane and the provincial team must deal with the uncertainties of the future with the growing need to administer social programs for the poor. Just as people's needs are increasing, the Sisters face more difficult challenges to their mission. Integrating Sisters and lay missionaries into the mission requires a capacity for persistence, creativity, and courage.

Historically, the the Congregation's Brazil Province has been dedicated to education and the mission to the people. The Missionaries of the Sacred Heart of Jesus arrived in São Paulo in 1903 and founded the Boni Consilii Educational Institution. It currently has 1,200 students, a large number of whom receive scholarships. Seventy percent of the students are approved to enter Brazil's highly competitive federal universitiesl.

In 1926, the Colégio Madre Cabrini was founded in São Paulo, and in 1949, work on the majestic building on Madre Cabrini Street, in Vila Mariana, was begun. The school surrounds a park of trees, flowers, and even gardens of edible crops planted by students. In addition to formal education activities, students take part in extracurricular activities such as music, ballet, theater, swimming, and various sports, as well as other educational activities during the school day.

The highly respected Regina Coeli High School has been educating students since 1928. Today it has 550 students.

The schools of the Province of Brazil are founded deeply on Mother Cabrini's pedagogy to "instruct the mind and form the heart for the exercise of citizenship." The goal is intellectual, religious, cultural, and social development for the building of a better world. Solid work is carried out by educators, students, and families aiming for the human and religious growth for social transformation and the promotion of life.

The Congregation also operates two programs for small children in São Paulo—the Centro Social da Criança (Children's Social Center) and Pequeno Príncipe (Little Prince).

The Centro Social was established to meet a dreadful need for child care in one of São Paulo's more challenging neighborhoods. It's on a little dead-end street just around the corner from an area known as Cracolândia. Crackland. In Cracolândia, drug addicts are free to engage in their addiction and all the related trafficking and other crimes. Police guard the streets going into the area. On one side of the police cordon, people trudge to work, walk their dogs, lug their shopping bags, and take their children down to the Centro Social. On the other side of the cordon, addicts squat on sidewalks and loll in makeshift tents as they partake of their illicit pleasures.

This is not to say that addicts and their associates don't come and go. They do. It's a pretty bad neighborhood. Right across the street from the Centro Social there's a little encampment of homeless people. But they're nice people. They get along with the Centro people. The homeless weren't the people who broke into the school four times in one year to steal computers, toys, and whatever else might have a resale value. The culprits, caught on a video surveillance tape, were teenagers. The Sisters showed the tape to the local gang boss. He recognized them. One was his nephew. He declared the Centro off limits and had the young burglars reeducated enough to put them in the hospital. He likes the Centro. His kid goes there.

The wider area is one of sweatshops, small shops, and tables on the sidewalk, all offering wares of the lowest possible price and quality. A large portion of the population in this area are immigrants from Bolivia, Peru, and Paraguay. Some of the people are veritable slaves given substandard wages (or no wages) and not being allowed to leave. They live in tenements where whole families share a windowless room and several families share one bathroom. Often there's no place to wash or dry clothes. It's a tough place to raise kids. Typically both parents (if there are two) have to work more than full time. Food is minimal, and no one has money for doctors, education, or child care. Often as not, parents take their kids to the sweatshops or to their retail table on the sidewalk. Sometimes the kids have to work; sometimes they're expected to just lie in a kind of stupor until it's time to go home. The Brazil Province opened the Centro Social to help children and their families in this difficult situation.

In the beginning the Centro was just a place to dump kids for the day. The place was small, and the personnel were too shorthanded to offer much constructive activity. Sisters and volunteers fed the kids, gave them love, and basically just kept them alive until their parents came to get them. But with financial support from outside sources and the municipal government, the Centro gradually expanded into four contiguous houses. Late 2016 saw 109 children enrolled, all free of charge. Space is still tight, but there's room for programs, festivals, games, naps, lunch, and so on. All twelve teachers have four-year college degrees in pedagogy. There are lots of toys and equipment around, enough mats for everyone to nap on. The municipal government pays salaries for teachers and staff, but there's just never enough money for all the things that could be done. But the city government, like every government in Brazil, is suffering financial shortfalls. The Sisters at the Centro fear the city might soon withdraw all financial support. That would be the end of the program.

Originally the school gave preference to the neediest families, but to receive municipal funding, it now has to use a lottery system for most admissions. Even though the Centro is in a bad neighborhood, people all over the city apply to get in, even professionals with enough money to send their children elsewhere. But simply because it's the closest nursery school around, a lot of the children are poor. Many of the mothers are young, often under twenty. One is just thirteen. Some of the mothers and their mothers both have children attending. Though coming from miserable living conditions, the children rarely appear to be mistreated beyond, of course, the inevitabilities of poverty, such as lack of time for parental guidance and affection. Generally the children are healthy, though one has Down syndrome and another is recovering from brain surgery. Sometimes a few are a little dirty, but that's because the parents simply have nowhere to bathe them. In such cases, the school day involves a bath. In all cases, it involves a good meal. And lots of love and guidance.

In another part of town, a peripheral area with a mixed population of middle and lower economic classes, the Congregation runs a larger nursery school, the Pequeno Príncipe. In late 2016 it was taking in 221 children from infancy to four years of age. Of the 22 teachers, all have university degrees and five have post-graduate degrees. Thanks to the higher economic level of families in the area, the Pequeno Príncipe is a little better financed than the Centro Social, so it offers a relatively sophisticated program. The children cycle through toy time, reading time, video time, music time, playground time, sit-in-the-sun time, manual dexterity time, and a blessed two-hour nap time when the whole school suddenly becomes quiet save for the pacifying music that plays softly in each room. And of course there's a whole lot of time dedicated to changing close to two hundred diapers each day.

The school operates on a philosophy of co-responsibility

Churches of People, Churches of Brick

with families. Parents and often grandparents are expected to participate in school activities such as dances, concerts, and festivals. The school doesn't teach religion per se—children of all religions are welcome—but Christian values and the Cabrini charism are infused in everything from lessons to attitudes. Though the children are barely at an age of self-consciousness and responsibility, the school is already developing them as whole human beings. Art, music, play, dexterity, social skills, clean diapers, and an ambience of love... It all adds up to good people.

* * *

The challenges in São Paulo extend throughout Brazil. Brazil's poorest state, Maranhão, way up in the northeast, is the polar opposite of São Paulo—rural, underdeveloped, and disorganized—but it suffers many of the same problems. It still has one foot back in the 19th century. There are still people who have no birth certificates, let alone shoes. Though the state has bountiful water resources, in many places water is scarce or brackish, and people lack the technology and infrastructure needed to produce something drinkable from whatever water nature provides. Manioc, rice, and wild fruits are the nutritional staples, though rice has become difficult to grow. Not long ago a family could grow enough to feed themselves and have some left over to sell. Now, due to climate change and worsening pests, they can't grow enough for their own needs. They also lack places to plant as agro-business takes more and more land from family farms. Existing large farms are just for cattle. The country's Plan of Agricultural Development is coming on like a devastating dragon. The objective is to turn the hinterland biome of the states of Maranhão, Tocantins, Piauí, and Bahia into a vast agricultural plantation of soy and eucalyptus. The plan might make the GDP look a little better, but it fails to take into account the people who live in that region.

Two MSCs—Eulália de Paiva Lima and Angélica dos Santos—live in a grubby highway settlement known as Troncamento, which means Crossroads, which is the only raison d'etre of the place. It's a relatively new settlement that used to be a large farm that wasn't producing anything. Just three years ago, after much struggle and resistance by local people, much of the land was redistributed to families. Restaurants, luncheonettes, tire shops, small stores, and little food shacks along the highway make up the basic economy for many families. Many families have no income other than the pensions of a retiree in the house or small "Bolsa Familia" welfare payments given to sustain poor families. Those who manage to keep a scrap of land do a little planting. The village smells of diesel fumes, smoldering trash, and the household waste water that trickles into street gutters. Troncamento, with a population of about five thousand, is actually part of the municipality of Itapecuru Mirim, which has some 65,000 people. That's where the high school is, though the school might as well be at the

Churches of People, Churches of Brick

North Pole since it's often not operating. In 2016, the mayor simply stopped paying municipal employees, so classes were sporadic and students lost an academic year of education. No one was cleaning the streets or providing other services essential to civilized life. The mayor also made over a million dollars disappear. Due to the weak state of Brazil's systems of justice and government, not much has been done to hold him accountable. In fact, despite numerous blatant scandals, he was reelected.

The dismal state of the economy, the government, the environment, and the climate leave Irmã Eulália and Sister Angélica with plenty to do. Sister Angélica's work is health organization and in homeopathic care with medicinal plants. Her work takes her to cities hours away. Her Organization for Public Health works out of a small garage that a family lets her use. It's divided into three spaces. The little waiting room has a few chairs made of rebar and plastic cord. The little office is a little desk and two chairs. The little back room holds an amazing array of homemade herbal medicines in recycled bottles. A crew of trained physiotherapists makes the various meds at home and brings them in.

Sister Angélica does her diagnosing at the little desk. She practices radiesthesia, the same mysterious principle behind dowsing rods. She uses a pendulum that she suspends over a patient's hand. As she points to pictures of parasites and microbes, the pendulum swings clockwise to affirm or counter-clockwise to deny that she's pointing to the right one. These parasites, she says, may go back several generations in the patient's family. Once the pendulum determines the cause of the health problem, she knows the area of the body that needs treatment. She tucks a selected semi-precious stone (hematite for kidneys, amethyst for the brain, emerald for lungs, and so on) under the hand and repeats the pendulum process to determine the right medicine and dosage.

Does it work? Ask the people who line up for treatment or who call her to the far sides of Maranhão or who claim to be cured of tuberculosis or freed from drug addiction. Ask the horse she cured of cancer. She herself says her treatments are one-hundred percent effective as long as the patient follows instructions precisely.

Irmã Eulália's work is mostly in spiritual guidance and social activism. She's relentless in trying to get people organized, to guide their Christian formation, and help them through social issues. One of those issues is securing land titles for quilombolas—descendants of slaves who have maintained quilombo communities, that is, communities of descendants of slaves who have preserved their cultural heritage. Though their people have lived where they are for more than a century and a half, their land is often claimed by absentee farmers or corporate interests.

Irmã Eulália was just seven years old when she knew she wanted to become a Missionary Sister. She was one of

Churches of People, Churches of Brick

twelve children in a family that lived in a place somewhat like Troncamento, but without the crossroads. It was the interior of Ceará, another rural, impoverished state of northeast Brazil. She was a little girl when the area suffered a terrible drought. Her family loaded their possessions onto two mules and headed 36 kilometers into the town of Quixeramobim. There they got a train to Fortaleza, the capital on the coast. At the time, the government was trying to help by shipping people down to Rio de Janeiro. The family spent fifteen days in the hold of a ship headed slowly south. In Rio, her father worked at various agricultural jobs. Little Eulália showed a lot of interest in learning and reading, but there was no school nearby. Her mother taught her the a-b-c's on scraps of paper torn from shopping bags. She didn't go to school until she was ten. When she was fourteen, her family sent her and three older sisters to the Colégio Regina Coeli, a good Catholic school in Vassouras, RJ. It was run by Missionary Sisters of the Sacred Heart. She became impassioned with the idea of a missionary life. She adored Madre Cabrini and the idea of traveling to faraway places to help people. But when she told her father that she wanted to become a Sister, he said *No*.

But when she turned eighteen, her father visited her at the school and said Yes. It was her life. She could do as she pleased. He would always be her father, and if religious life didn't work out, she could always come home.

It worked out. She entered the novitiate in the state of Rio

Grande do Sul at the southern tip of Brazil. She took her first vows in 1964. She was hoping to get assigned to France, which she'd heard was a nice place, but the Congregation sent her to the school in Rio Pomba, Minas Gerais. There she taught mathematics and Portuguese even as she continued to study for a teaching certificate. Then she went to teach at her alma mater in Vassouras, then to São Paulo to pursue a degree in mathematics. She then returned to Vassouras to teach, but within three years, she felt a disturbing dissatisfaction. Was she going to spend her whole life teaching math?

Then one day Father Daniel Tomassia, of the Congregation of the Most Holy Redeemer, visited the school. He told the community about missions in the interior of Bahia and a request from one diocese to open a new mission there. Her heart burned to go, but she felt a duty to continue her current mission. Who would teach her classes? The Congregation didn't have funds to hire teachers.

A mission was opened in 1972 by two other Sisters. Late that year, the Provincial Superior visited the school and called Irmã Eulália into the office. Eulália was scared. What had she done wrong? But apparently the Provincial had spoken with the priest. She asked Irmã Eulália if she'd like to take a mission in Remanso, Bahia. Eulália said, "But how could I? Who would take over my classes? I don't know anything about parochial work. All I know how to do is teach."

The Provincial said. "No. You can do more than that. We can find a teacher from outside the congregation. Our work is to be missionaries among the people."

Other Sisters thought maybe she wasn't too wise to be taking all her college education into the outback where most people couldn't even read and where life was anything but cushy. But Irmã Eulália didn't want cushy. She wanted to work with people who needed help.

So off she went to the Diocese of Juazeiro—not the city but to a Cabrini mission some two hundred kilometers (120 miles) away, in Remanso. She thought that was pretty outback, but that was just the jumping off point. From there a priest took her a hundred kilometers (sixty miles) by Jeep, an arduous four-hour trip down a poor excuse for a road to the village of Campo Alegre de Lourdes.

And there, she says, she began her real novitiate experience, her real introduction to the word of God in the Bible, her experience with God, her real vocation to religious life. There her dynamic conscience was strengthened. There the true meaning of consecrated religious life matured. There she was in the middle of so many conflicts and challenges—as much from the Congregation as from the local political power. It was an apprenticeship within a spiritual conflict. The diocese helped with the formative moments of the mission, giving all support and incentive to the Sisters. The Word of God was the light and logic of the mission.

Irmã Eulália was part of the Cabrini community in Remanso. Every week she spent three days there, then returned to Campo Alegre. For two years she moved from house to house, family to family. It was a powerful way to get to know the community and the seriousness of the situation. The village was under extreme duress—poverty and oppression from those who governed the state and the town. The people were submissive, threatened, and afraid of the authorities.

Then the priest who worked there was sent to the Amazon. By special request from the bishop, Pope John-Paul II granted Irmã Eulália the power to give the sacraments. She accepted responsibility for the next seven years, approaching the community with that Cabrinian grace that transcends humility and boldness. It brought to her mind Exodus Chapter 3, where God tells Moses, "put off thy shoes from off thy feet, for the place whereon thou standest is sacred ground." That's how Irmã Eulália felt as she worked in the parched and impoverished community of people under duress. She was on sacred ground.

Over the next five years, the drought worsened. Fathers had to leave their families to go look for work in São Paulo, Rio, or Brasilia. They expected to return when the rains returned, but the drought continued year after year. People became more desperate. Sacred ground or not, the land of milk and honey was beyond anyone's dreams. They could barely get a swallow of water. The town hired people to dig basins to collect rainwater, but the work was excruciating for pathetic amounts of water. And this work was given only to people who supported the government and not the ecclesiastical work of the Cabrini Sisters. Remanso and other communities were ignored. The municipal government was supposed to be sending a water

Churches of People, Churches of Brick

truck to the village twice a week, but it didn't even come once a week. The so-called "colonels" and land barons who essentially owned the government and most of the land had other intentions for municipal funds. The rule of law was a tenuous concept. This was during the years of Brazil's military dictatorship, which had little interest in the problems of rural areas. Irmã Eulália did what she could to defend people's rights. The politicians were calling her a cobra de saia...a skirt snake. The bishop, D. José Rodrigues de Souza, stood with the Sisters, but they didn't feel they were getting the same support from their congregational Province. The Province didn't seem to understand the significance and difficulty of religious life inserted among the people in the defense and promotion of life. It was more concerned about the strictly religious aspect, not the pastoral. This led to many conflicts. It was said that struggling for life, for land, for rights, was not in the Congregation's charism. Some in the Province in São Paulo and Rio felt that the mission couldn't even be considered a mission of the Province. It was just a Sister working independently.

Then, suddenly, the Provincial Superior called Irmã Eulália back to São Paulo. For the good of the Congregation, she explained, the emphasis was going to be on developing the projects that provided financial stability and helped sustain the Congregation. Schools, in other words, rather than pastoral work out in the middle of nowhere.

Eulália resisted. She had too many projects in the works, too many people depending on her. Again, Exodus 3 came to mind: "And the Lord said, I have surely seen the affliction of my people which are in Egypt, and have heard their cry by reason of their taskmasters; for I know their sorrows." She heard her people's cry. She knew their sorrows. She did not want to leave them.

But she also knew she'd taken a vow of obedience. Under great pressure, she asked for a year off from the Congregation so she could continue to work with her poor, suffering people. She could not leave them. They saw her as strength and hope, someone on their side, the presence of a Church in solidarity with the poor and forgotten.

During this year of detachment from the Province, cut off from the world and struggling against a terrible drought, it was hard for her to discern whether to return to the Congregation after that year. The problems were many, and the cry for justice had never been greater. She had no time to think about whether to go back to São Paulo or not. Rather, she thought about how to respond to that inhuman situation in which she found her people. But one day toward the end of the year, in prayer, she knew: yes, she would go back.

She went to Vassouras for a year of discernment. But she wasn't one to remain cloistered in prayer and thought. She continued to support the struggle of the rural poor. She was active with the Comissão Pastoral da Terra (CPT), an organization founded by the National Conference of Bishops of Brazil to support and defend the rights of rural workers and landless farmers. In Sapucaia, she was active in the rural workers union and in the organization of communities hit by the construction of four dams on the Rio Paraiba do Sul. Though political protest was traditionally outside the realm of religious work, she participated in demonstrations against the military government. During her whole missionary life, she was integrated with the CPT. The CPT contributed to her formation in sociology, law, theology, and history in courses given to rural workers. During her vacation time, she went to the CPT to study pastoral theology.

Irmã Eulália had a major impact on the Congregation when she met General Superior Maria Barbagallo, who was visiting Rio de Janeiro. Suor Maria had spent many years working with the poor in Central America. She'd always been a big believer in the importance of MSCs being inserted in communities. She was no stranger to military governments and political strife. The two Sisters had a lot to talk about. Irmã Eulália told Suor Maria that the Sisters in Brazil didn't seem to understand the charism of Madre Cabrini as it regarded activism and commitment to the defense of life. Suor Maria told Irmã Eulália that she'd been through the same struggle. She felt the same way about social activism. She agreed that Eulália was a Sister who should be inserted in a community, not teaching at an urban high school.

Looking ahead to the next General Chapter meeting, Suor Maria wanted to better understand how insertion in Brazil worked. The insertion experience had taken big strides in Brazil, but only with some confusion for the Sisters involved. It needed to be clarified so more conflicts didn't arise. Suor Maria called together the Sisters of Brazil, Central America, and Argentina to meet in Buenos Aires. There they discussed their various experiences. Later, the group was called to another meeting at the Congregation's house in Codogno, Italy, with Sisters from Europe and the United States. The objective was to raise points to be included in a document on the nature and importance of insertion. Suor Maria pulled all the thoughts into a document and presented it for discussion at the General Chapter meeting of 1996. The document made it clear that if the Congregation continued to become a self-perpetuating institution rather than an active part of communities, it would lose its purpose and it would die.

By 1994 the Congregation had been out of Brazil's trouble-plagued Northeast for almost ten years. The Northeast was the most disregarded, abandoned, and mistreated region of Brazil, and it was time for Cabrini Sisters to go back. The Provincial Superior, Sister Alzira Maria Marin, delegated Sisters Suany and Eulália to visit the diocese that were asking for a Cabrini presence. In the next year, three communities of Sisters and Lay Missionaries were established.

Cabrini Lay Missionaries were becoming increasingly important. The Solidariedade Missionária Cabriniana (SOMISCA) was established to be a strong lay missionary presence in communities. Missions were established in the states of Piauí, Ceará, Maranhão, and Bahia. Each mission was (and is) dedicated to people's struggle to survive as individuals, as communities, and as Christians. With that goal in common, each mission was unique in its response to local needs. Irmã Eulália herself served in several places before landing in Troncamento, Maranhão.

Eulália arrived in Troncamento with no intention of being tied down to Sisterly assistance with masses, baptisms, weddings, funerals and sacraments. Yes, she's involved in those things, too, but she feels compelled to go deeper into the community, down to the roots of human problems. And if there was ever a place that needed someone like her, it's Troncamento. It's an intersection of problems. The two highways that meet there carry everything that gets trucked into or out of the state capital, São Luiz, a port down on the coast. Inevitably the traffic has come to include drugs and humans. It isn't just the marijuana of years past, a natural drug which Irmã Eulália would just as soon see legalized as a homeopathic medicine. In recent years the drugs have come to include cocaine and crack. Local youth, having little to do and not much hope for the future, indulge in the drugs' temporary escape. Drug use and distribution has led inexorably to crime—not just theft and prostitution but murder. The police aren't up to the job, and anyway, drug-related crime isn't the kind of thing police can really resolve. It's a social problem. A spiritual problem.

But highway traffic isn't the only problem going through town. The town, like many others across the state, is also sliced in half by a railroad owned by Vale, the giant mining company. Trains haul huge amounts of iron ore from the vast hematite mine at Carajás down to São Luiz. Trains three hundred cars long barrel down the tracks almost every hour, and they take almost an hour to pass. They don't stop for anything, and they don't carry passengers. They serve corporate purposes only. The impact on communities is of no corporate interest. Vale is required to listen to communities, which include villages of Native Americans and quilombos, communities that were founded by fugitive slaves. If Vale listens to towns and communities, it barely hears the message.

Crossing the tracks by foot, car, or farm wagon is dangerous and often requires a long wait. Vale was been slow and reluctant to deal with such issues. In fact the company long ignored the problems until the people of the quilombo Itapecuru and other groups decided to work together to solve their common problem—something that doesn't come naturally to them. They set up camp right on the tracks and refused to move until Vale agreed to certain improvements. The company was decent enough not to run them over. After five days—three of them on hunger strike—and millions of dollars in lost revenues, the company agreed to build some overpasses and pay for infrastructure projects, such as water systems, in various villages. The overpasses got built, but unfortunately the mayor of Itapecuru Mirim "diverted" the money, and the projects never got done.

It was a victory not just because of the overpasses but because people had successfully stood up to one of the world's largest corporations. Even more important, they had come together and gotten organized and done something for the

Churches of People, Churches of Brick

common good. Pro-active cooperation is not a tradition in the interior of Maranhão. The tradition is to mind your own business, presume that nothing can be done, and suffer problems as an unalterable part of life.

Irmã Eulália's fundamental mission is to change that way of thinking, to develop a political awareness oriented on looking for human rights that are being denied. She wants to form people to be aware of all aspects of life—social, economic, biblical, religious, and cultural—and to understand how all that relates to public policies. Such a cultural and psychological shift isn't impossible. The people in the 52 communities she works with are hard-working and good-hearted. Everyone knows everyone, and they all get along. If asked for help, they gladly give it. But will they recognize a common problem and get together to solve it? Not without someone motivating them. Maybe they resign themselves to passivity because of the despair that comes with poverty and exclusion. Maybe it goes back to the days of slavery, when initiative was a sin, not a virtue. Maybe it's a tendency to wait for the government to come along and solve the problem. But little by little, they are learning. Irmã Eulália is showing them what they can do if they try, if they work together as a community. To make that happen, she's always looking for and nurturing leaders. Even if the project is merely to organize a local festival, when someone takes charge, they see themselves as leaders and they learn something about the power of their community.

But of course community action is needed for a lot more

than festivals. It's the need to struggle against corruption, land-grabbing, bad sanitation, preventable diseases, wells drying up, drug addiction, inadequate schools, unemployment, malnutrition...so many problems that make each other worse. There is so much to do and way too few people willing to get up and do it unless a certain Sister comes around and tells them they should do it, and, more important, they can do it.

In recent years, Protestant evangelical churches have been putting down roots in the area. In 2016 there were more than 19 different Protestant organizations around Troncamento. Some are well intentioned. Some are fly-by-night. Irmã Eulália sees them as offering people little more than the basic sacraments, not helping in the struggle to deal with their harsh reality. Their limited practice of the Gospel fails to heed Christ's call for action in defense of dignity, decency, and human rights.

Irmã Eulália is very much the face of today's Catholicism. She is very much the embodiment of St. Teresa of Ávila, whose poetic prayer drives home the message that "Christ has no body now but yours/ No hands, no feet on earth but yours..." The Church that was once the opiate of the masses has become the opposite: a friend, counselor, and helping-hand of masses that need to be shaken up and spurred to action.

Unfortunately, Irmã Eulália doesn't have a helicopter. Getting to 52 communities at the far ends of dirt roads isn't easy. But little by little, she is recruiting leaders, activists, and concerned citizens. One, Aurelina, a young woman from one of the communities, lives with Eulália and Angélica as an experience that may be her first step toward becoming an MSC. She's struggling to graduate from a high school that's closed too often for her to finish courses. When she's free, she and other Catholic workers knock on doors at a given community, bringing palpable solidarity to each family. They ask if everything's all right. They ask what they can do. They carry Christ's call for action right there to the door.

* * *

The state bordering Maranhão to the south and east, Piauí, ties with Maranhão for the title of "poorest state in Brazil." The capital, Teresina, sits between two rivers—the Poti and the Parnaíba— that separate the two states. The population of Teresina is about 900,000, many of whom are migrants from the rural areas of Piauí and other states. With poor perspectives for housing, employment and education, migrants have flooded to the outskirts of Teresina. But they arrived with no money for homes.

On June 3, 1998, people decided to do something about their homelessness and landlessness. It was the day of the Santa Cruz dos Milagres, when an iconic cross is brought to various towns in Piauí. It's a religious event accompanied by a festival that includes a kind of rodeo. The rodeo involves cowboys on horseback trying to grab a bull by its tail and pull it off its feet. The event also involves a lot of betting and drinking and social events. A good time is had by all except the bull.

It's a popular event enjoyed by just about everyone, but that year, not everyone was there. Some seven thousand homeless peasants were poised at the edge of fifty hectares of unused land. The land was owned by a farmer with vast holdings, but it was unused, covered by trees and scrub. The peasants had been organized by the Federation of Associations of Residents and Community Councils (FAMCC) of Piaui with the support of the Movimento dos Sem Terras (MST, an organization dedicated to securing land for landless workers), the Comissão Pastoral da Terra (CPT, a Church organiztion dedicated to helping poor rural people), and other social movements.

Somehow all these people managed to keep a really big secret. No one suspected that shortly after dark, while the ranchers and landowners were watching the rodeo, a horde of people was going to move onto the land. Each carried a machete in one hand, a flashlight in the other, and, according to myth, a Bible under the arm.

Very quietly, very quickly, they swarmed across the land, hacking down brush and trees, setting up tents, gathering wood, starting cooking fires, digging latrines. By the time the sun rose, they were an encampment. It looked like they'd been there for years. Depending on which side of an ideological chasm Brazilians are on, such an action is called either an occupation or an invasion. By whatever name, it was a tense situation that was bound to involve violence. And it did. Police came in and drove people out, but most managed to hold their ground. A tide of violence went back and forth several times, sweeping people out only to have them return. In the end, the people remained.

The new encampment was soon known as Vila Irmã Dulce in honor of a Brazilian Catholic missionary, Dulce Lopes Pontes. Irmã Dulce is also known as "the good angel of Bahia" because of her charity and love for people most in need.

The occupation meant land was available for anyone who claimed it. More and more migrants arrived. The population swelled in size and expanded across the land. It became the second largest urban land occupation in the history of Brazil. But it was a shaky situation. The poverty was absolute. Government services—water, sewers, electricity, schools—were minimal to nil. The Church had yet to establish a presence of faith and action.

The Archbishop at the time, Dom Miguel Câmara, called on the Missionary Sisters of the Sacred Heart to witness and insert themselves into the reality of the situation. The most immediately available missionaries were Sister Denise Alves Morra and Sister Laudir Inês Crocolli. They lived in Piauí but some four hundred kilometers (250 miles) away in the small town of Pimenteiras. It was a very remote, rural, semi-arid area with few phones, and no direct bus service to the capital. A priest came through only once a year for festivals for patron saints. The Sisters, who were active in the many communities in the region, had been there for three years when the Archbishop called them to Teresina for the emergency situation at Vila Irmã Dulce.

In early 2000, at the request of Father Demerval Brasil, the

Pimenteiras mission was moved to Vila Irmã Dulce. The Sisters were responsible for the evangelization of the urban confusion of the encampment. At the same time, they worked on pastoral catechism with children and young adults. They heard the laments of the women at the only water well, which had been dug by the diocese. They worked on the social organization of the Vila. They helped lay out streets with lengths of string. They helped illiterate people get important documents, such as birth certificates and identity cards. They helped with the formation of the Associations of Residents and the struggle for schools, health clinics, and nursery schools where parents could leave children. They inspired people to demand their right to water, electricity, and phone service. With the financial aid of ADVENIAT and the involvement of the Catholic Community, with barn-raising spirit of community cooperation, they got a church built. It was dedicated to the Sacred Heart of Jesus.

Everybody at Vila Irmã Dulce needed help, but it was children who needed it most. Parents, desperate for work, had to leave their kids somewhere during the day. All of the kids were hungry, and many were malnourished. Home life was tough on these kids. The vast majority of families were sustained by a single mother. If there was a man present, it probably wasn't the children's father. Sexual and psychological abuse was rampant. Children needed a safe place to spend their days.

At first the Sisters took in children just to keep them off the street. Until they could get a building built, they established their daycare center in the shade of a tree. Little by little they

Churches of People, Churches of Brick

started offering programs, orientation, catechism, and food. A few women sympathetic to the cause, impressed with the Sisters' efforts at evangelization, came to know the Cabrinian charism a little better. With the help of these Cabrini Lay Missionaries, the Centro Juventude Santa Cabrini—The Saint Cabrini Youth Center—was born. The Sisters purposefully used the title "Santa" to differentiate the Center as a Catholic space. The Congregation's Province of Brazil soon sent the Vila some young women who were preparing to be Sisters along with Sister Inês Caixeta, who had worked with Irmã Denise in the Maré slum in Rio de Janeiro, Irmã Ursolina Vicenzi, Irmã Roseni Teresinha Gonçalves and Irmã Angelica dos Santos. A few years later, the young women were transferred to the Piauí town of Oeiras.

Today, the Center is the main MSC operation in Teresina. It is also a model of social action for the municipal government, demonstrating how social programs should be organized. The Sisters develop political strategies and promote solidarity throughout the missionary projects. They also establish partnerships with the public and private sectors in harmony with the promotion and defense of the rights of children and young adults in the community.

Today the Centro serves two hundred children and adolescents and some fifty young adults. In all, counting parents and other family members, over a thousand people get involved in a given month. The Center isn't a school, but its mission involves the education of the heart in accordance with Cabrinian pedagogy. Its programs range from capoeira (a vigorous, athletic dance derived from an obsolete martial art) to critical thinking and environmental awareness. Salaried and volunteer staff teach values that many homes have forgotten under the pressures of poverty. Dedicated to developing people in all their dimensions, the Center is open to all children regardless of religious affiliation. A large number of the children are Protestant or Pentacostals. The Center celebrates the major Christian and Cabrinian holidays, but there's no main focus on catechism.

The families involved in the Centro are a tiny minority of the thousands of young people in the Vila. They are among the few who get to experience an alternative to a street life that is increasingly dominated by drug trafficking and the violence that inevitably accompanies it. That illicit street life dominates the local culture and economy. If a boy in the area is asked what he'd like to be when he grows up, odds are he'll say he wants to work in the trafficking of narcotics. It's the most immediate economic opportunity and one of few visible local sources of employment.

Gangs and the drug trade have changed life in the Vila drastically and dreadfully. In the first years after the initial occupation, people saw each other as fellow travelers, brothers and sisters in a common effort to own a home and lead a decent life. Houses had no walls around them, and people took chairs out into the streets at night to sit around talking and watching their kids play. Today, everyone is behind locked doors shortly

Churches of People, Churches of Brick

after sunset. Deaths by gunfire and the settling of criminal issues are commonplace. The Sisters have had no choice but to put a wall around the Centro. The wall is topped with barbed wire and electric fencing. The Center has always been respected by the local criminals. In fact, some of the gangsters send their kids there. But in late 2016, two people managed to get over the fence and make off with some valuable items. Thanks to the oversight of the Sacred Heart of Jesus, a surveillance camera, and anonymous informants, the Sisters know where they could go to buy their things back, but they have preferred not to risk their lives. It was risky enough just to report the theft to the police. They showed the police the invasion happening on the surveillance video. They told the police where they could find the TV, and they identified the culprits by name. For reasons unknown, the police showed no interest. The incident illustrates the riskiness of opting to do the work of Jesus and also the insecurity experienced by everyone who lives in the peripheries of big cities.

Bishop Jacinto Brito has warned the Sisters to be careful. He doesn't want them taking chances or presuming themselves untouchable by crime. His warning brought to mind something that the warm and beloved Dom Luciano Mendes once told them: "Love has to be smart."

One "smart love" thing the Sisters have done is organize a monthly event called Cabrini in the Streets, something like the "Prayer Festivals" that Madre Cabrini once organized. At least once a month, the Sisters and some volunteers section off a few streets and hold socialization and evangelization events. Kids get a rare chance to play outdoors at night, the way kids used to. The unobstructed growth of gangs is only part of a generally worsening situation. A neoliberal federal government is whittling away at family support programs. A new constitutional amendment has frozen spending on education, social programs, and virtually every other part of government spending for the next twenty years, guaranteeing that public education will go from bad to worse. Big economic projects are being pushed with the promise of new jobs, but in reality, they are a plan for the desertification caused by a massive planting of eucalyptus for pulp across the interior of Maranhão, Piauí, and Bahia. The planting will eliminate any possibility of small family farms. Greater migration into cities is inevitable. So is environmental devastation. A new railroad line across the Northeast will bring progress at the cost of devastating the environment and sacrificing people and local communities across the interior of Piaui state. The swelling tide of poverty and problems will make the social services of the Centro Juventude Santa Cabrini all the more essential in the face of a population losing faith and hope.

Irmãs Denise and Glória are aware that the Center will never be able to solve all the problems that surround them. But they also know that they are making a difference through witnessing and following Jesus and engaging in public policies. They are intelligent, active, concerned women religious devoted to transforming the reality around them. They actively participate in forming public policy with the municipal government. Irmã Denise is president of the Municipal Council for Social Assistance. Irmã Glória is secretary of the Municipal Council on the Rights of Children and Adolescents. Their work on these councils involves governmental and nongovernmental organizations, and it requires a lot of time. The missionaries contribute to the forming of municipal laws, analyses of projects, and the monitoring of public policies, especially those for children and adolescents. To better meet the challenge of social assistance, the Sisters went back to college to become better qualified.

They are also involved in an organization called A Cry for Life, which was created by the Conference of Religious in Brazil. It's the Brazilian part of an international network of organizations that fight human trafficking. Through workshops in schools, A Cry for Life educates young people on what human trafficking is, how it happens, and how to avoid it. It's a real problem. Children are trafficked all over Brazil. In Piauí, many young people get tricked with false promises of employment only to end up cutting sugar cane or timber in other states. Some end up prostituted on the streets in distant cities.

The Center is generally run by dedicated Cabrini Lay Missionaries. Senhora Fernanda Campelo Mattos is Auxiliary Coordinator of the Center and has been actively involved in the settling and development of the Vila since the very first day of the occupation. She lived right at the edge of the place where it happened. She awoke in the morning and was astonished to see tents up everywhere, cooking smoke in the air, a vast encampment where there had been woods the day before. It was amazing, and it looked like trouble. She couldn't do much more than offer a little food and a garden hose where people could come get water. She was there when the police came in and knocked everything down and the people came back and settled in again. It was when the Missionary Sisters arrived that she knew things were going to start changing for the better. She found a garage with a room attached where the Sisters could stay when they first arrived at the Vila.

Fernanda had never known nuns like this. The one's she'd known were calm, quiet, passive, turned inward in prayer. The MSCs came in and took charge. They were prayer with action, dynamic and driven and unwilling to accept impossibility. They were concerned not just with faith and food but human rights and human development. If she'd known Sisters could be like that, she thinks now, she might have opted for the religious life. It was too late for vows of chastity, obedience, and poverty—she had a husband and children—but she could still lend a hand. She lent a lot of hand. People started calling her Fernanda Cabrini. She was part of the Centro before it was a Centro, back when it was under a big tree, the children coming in three shifts.

Then one day the Congregation invited her and four other especially dedicated volunteers—Alcioneia, Freitas, Aparecida, and Meiriele—to deepen their Cabrinian charism. She could hardly believe the honor and opportunity. For the next two years, the four women went to conferences and retreats to prepare to be consecrated as Lay Missionaries. They attended a Chapter meeting in Italy—a rare privilege in that it is uncommon for Religious Congregations to include laity at their Chapters. They learned how to live the charism by contributing to the spiritual and human formation of everyone around them.

Fernanda became Auxiliary Coordinator of the Centro Social. Today she earns a salary, but when her salaried day is over, she becomes a CLM working as a volunteer. The paid work and volunteer work blur into the total dedication that distinguishes the Cabrini charism. She says that if for some reason the Centro closed, she'd still be a Lay Missionary, and even if the Cabrini Lay Missionary program ended, she says she'd still live the Cabrini charism. It isn't something you can just leave behind, she says. It's so lovely and so deep.

* * *

In Rio de Janeiro, the Vila do João is a housing project constructed by the federal government's Projeto Rio urban development program in the early 1980s. The building of the Vila was controversial because it aimed to remove people from swampy, tidal lowlands where they lived in abject conditions. A third of the inhabitants of the Maré area were living in houses on stilts, mainly in the communities known as Baixa do Sapateiro and Parque Maré. After some resistance, the inhabitants were moved to the Vila do João. It was a neighborhood of five-story apartment buildings and prefabricated houses near

Rio's Guanabara Bay. The Vila was named after the military-appointed president of Brazil at that time, General João Baptista de Oliveira Figueiredo. It's alongside the Avenida Brasil and Linha Amarela thoroughfares, near the slums of Conjunto Esperança, Salsa e Merengue (Novo Pinheiro), and Vila do Pinheiro.

Under a succession of corrupt state and municipal governments, the neighborhood was neglected. Building codes were ignored. To squeeze more families into the houses, precarious second and third stories got added and fronts got bumped out onto sidewalks. The electrical system became a thicket of jury-rigged wires illegally tapping off the grid. Trees along the creeks got cut down as houses were built on rickety concrete piles. Waste water flowed through PVC pipes right into the water. Garbage collection was daily but still not adequate, so trash got thrown into creeks and left on sidewalks. It produced a most disturbing odor and attracted rats and roaches. During heavy rains, the trash and sewage flowed up from the creeks and into the streets.

As in most slums in Rio, Vila do João became dominated by traffickers in drugs and weapons. The area had natural boundaries that made it hard for police to patrol. The only effective access points are off Avenida Brasil and Linha Amarela. Teenagers with AK-47s guard the entrances. People are free to come in to buy drugs, but they have to stop at the checkpoint, then proceed with windows open and headlights off. They have to drive over a long series of speed bumps meant to slow down police on their occasional "operations." Kids with walkie-talkies on every street corner monitor all traffic. Outsiders are expected to stop at any of many tables set up on sidewalks. Stacked with drugs, the tables are guarded by more kids with machine guns. Shoppers are expected to purchase the pharmaceuticals of their predilection, and then leave. The only drug not available is crack. The gang in control at present, the TCP (Terceiro Comando Puro—the Third Pure Command) prohibits both sale and use of that one drug. Any residents caught using it are given a matter of minutes to leave Vila do João. (They won't have to go far. The neighboring district, controlled by a less civil-minded gang, will have what they need.)

Madre Cabrini would see this place as prime real estate for a mission. It's a frontier of the poor and people who have been excluded from the neoliberal system. That's how Irmã Roseni Teresinha Gonçalves sees the situation. She is one of few people who can drive right through the checkpoint with a little wave. She can park her car across the street from the Projeto Social Santa Cabrini. She can leave it unlocked. No one is going to mess with it. Not on purpose anyway. It's been hit by bullets four times during police "operations," but they weren't really aiming at her car. It was just in the way. Other than that, she's had no problems. The Projeto gets hit, too, during the occasional shoot-outs between police and traffickers.

The Projeto Social Cabrini cares for about a hundred children from six to twelve years of age. They are from the Vila do João and nearby communities. The children feel safe there, and families trust the work of the Missionary Sisters of the Sacred Heart of Jesus. If a gunfight starts while they're painting pictures, discussing human values, or enjoying a nutritious lunch, they know the drill. They move low under the windows into an interior space where they do some other activity until things outside settle down. (Public schools, on the other hand, dismiss all students at the sound of a single gunshot. Absurdly, all the children are sent home, which means they have to go out into the streets where the shooting is happening, and most of them aren't actually able to go home because their parents are out working.)

The mission to the Vila began in the 1980s with Irmãs Florência Victor Rodrigues, Joana Amélia Soares, and Iracema Resende. In the 1990s, Irmã Glória and Irmã Denise—the same who were later given the mission in Teresina—arrived. They lived in the house where the Projeto is today. The Vila was burgeoning with poor migrants coming south from the impoverished, drought-stricken Northeast. A parish community center, the Centro Social Beato José de Anchieta, had been built nearby under the direction of Irmã Florência, but it wasn't enough for tens of thousands of people. Following the philosophy of Madre Cabrini, Irmãs Denise and Glôria continued the work of the Sisters who had preceded them. First they built a "church of people"—a community of people working together—and then a "church of brick"—a place to worship. It was a nice place to worship, an octagonal church made of brick. The Sisters were approved as vicars so that they could administer sacraments. Eventually a priest was assigned to the area. He had a larger church built. It looks a lot like warehouse, but at least it's got plenty of room. The Sisters backed off and got down to what they did best: social work. Irmãs Albertina G. Goulart, Inês Caixeta de Silva, and Maria Aparecida de Fátima joined them.

The Projeto Social began its activities as part of the Obra Social Santa Cabrini in 2000 in the parish's Centro Social Beato José de Anchieta community center. Within five years, however, the Congregation had to close the MSC house because of worsening violence. The Projeto Social was moved to the house where it is now. The Sisters running the program were Alzira Maria Marin and Lourdes Colloda, both working out of the Obra Social Santa Cabrini (Saint Cabrini Social Project) that was and still is at the building complex Madre Cabrini bought in 1908 in the much more gentle and gentrified neighborhood in Tijuca. Irmã Roseni arrived in 2013. She commutes from Tijuca to the Projeto Social in Vila do João every morning unless she gets a phone call advising her that there's a protracted gunfight going on. In the afternoon, she returns to Tijuca. There, with the help of 24 collaborators and Lay Missionaries, she administers the Obra Social (Social Project)program for adults, young adults, and elderly people. They knit, crochet, work with computers, do crafts, play games, dance, discuss the Bible, pray, go out, have fun, eat well, and take care of each other. They experience love.

Irmã Roseni is the only Sister who dares to come into Vila do João. All the volunteers and staff who work at the project live in the Vila. That's part of the Cabrini philosophy, to hire local in order to support the local economy. One of the staff, Ana Paula, was once one of the kids at the Projeto. It built the foundation of her life, a life that could have easily drifted in another direction. She was a kid and then a volunteer and then worked her way up to Director of the Projeto. Now she's off to Denmark for post-graduate work.

Today the Projeto Social Santa Cabrini works with about a hundred children. Its motto is "Alicerçando Vidas"—Founding Lives. Except for the public schools and a municipal health clinic, it is the only social services agency in the Vila do João, which now has a population estimated at 40,000. The children come in two shifts of fifty. Their days include a meal better than anything they're likely to get at home, and workshops that teach them things they aren't likely to learn at home. They do reading and then apply critical thinking to discussions. They dance and sing, sometimes striving to make themselves heard over the big boom-box down the street at the sidewalk drugstore. They learn to play musical instruments. They practice capoeira. They work with computers. They feel safe and loved in this Cabrinian mission.

Most important, they learn about human values, which is not something commonly present or practiced in Vila do João. Families have disintegrated to the point where weary single mothers working two or more jobs are trying to raise children in one-room apartments called "kitchenettes." Houses that were built for one family often house as many as nine, all sharing one

Churches of People, Churches of Brick

bathroom. If there's a man living with the mother, he's rarely the children's father. By necessity, very young children are often left locked in the kitchenette—five-year-olds babysitting three-year-olds—all day long while their mother is out trying to scrape up enough money to feed them. Schools are often closed, maybe just because the teacher never showed up, so kids are left to wander the streets. The social environment is steeped in values anything but human: religion disregarded as an irrelevant relic, drugs as an escape, drug trafficking as the best job around, violence as a way of doing business, punk music all around, gangsters respected as some kind of community leaders.

In a sad, sick way, the gangsters are community leaders. At least they maintain order, which in many areas of Rio is more than the municipal government does. In fact, Vila do João is one of the safest places in Rio de Janeiro. Theft and violence inside the Vila is not tolerated. All movement in the streets is monitored. Thievery is punished summarily and brutally. If a woman complains that her husband has beaten her, the gang leadership will send someone over to deliver a message by breaking some of his bones. The drug trade is carefully regulated. Though young teens may be patrolling with semi-automatic pistols, they dare not abuse the privilege. Once a kid jumped out in front of Sister Roseni's car, pointed a pistol at her and demanded that she stop and explain herself. She gave him a look. Then his radio crackled and central command told him to leave her alone, she's the Sister. As she drove away, she saw him getting beaten down for his impropriety.

Some people like to say that the TCP gang is an alternative government. If so, it's one that leaves the essentials of civility—water, sewerage, power, education, health, postal system—to the other government. The urban infrastructure is maintained and essential services are provided by the other government, but only with permission from the gang. When the gang leaders decide to hold a community dance, it simply informs a public school that it will have to close that Friday so the gym can be decorated for the dance. The gang can also shut down a street for a festival. In fact, when Sister Roseni wants to have an outdoor event for Christmas caroling or a little festival in front of the Projeto, she can ask the TCP to close it off. And that is all she will ask of the gangsters. She does not want their money.

Money is her biggest problem. The Projeto Social doesn't generate any revenue. Its services are free. It isn't a school, so it doesn't receive any support from the city. It used to get grants from companies, but with the economic downturn, there are none available. Funding used to come from Cabrini schools in São Paulo, Vassouras, and Rio Pomba, but after a change in law, not-for-profit schools are limited in how much they can send to other projects. There used to be some funding from a clinic the Congregation had in Tijuca, but the law prevents not-for-profits from offering more than two kinds of service. The Congregation preferred to stay in education and social services, so the clinic closed. The Centro Social in Teresina and the Obra Social in Rio cost over a quarter million dollars a year to operate. Soon one of the two may have to close—probably the Projeto, the small and only hope for a handful of children among thousands in a violent slum in a corrupt city in a bankrupt state in a nation bereft of optimism. The charism is there, the will, the need and the spirit are there, but the money is not.

Sister Lucy Panettieri

Walking on Sacred Ground

When does a girl begin to become a Sister? When does she begin the process of formation? With a whisper from God? With a conversation that touches her soul? With something in the world that touches her heart?

For little Lucy Panettieri, it began at an age almost too young to remember. She was born in Sicily to an Italian father and an American mother, though her mother had been in Italy since childhood. Times were a little hard in Sicily, and Lucy's father was disenchanted with farming. He wanted to go to America. For reasons of visa, his American-born wife and his 14 year old daughter, who was considered an American citizen, went first. Lucy was just five. She had to stand on a dock as her mother boarded an ocean liner, waved good-bye, and sailed away. Lucy cried the way only five-year-olds can cry. Her remaining family had to hold her back from running off the dock and into the water to get back to her mother.

That was the trauma—a seemingly insufferable loss, though it was only temporary. After some intercontinental complications, the family was reunited in Chicago. The only one missing was a sister who remained in Sicily, where she was a nun. Mr. Panettieri got a job at Cabrini's Columbus Hospital. After an unsatisfying experience at public school, Lucy was enrolled at St. Michael Grammar School, just a couple of blocks away. From around that time, she knew she wanted to be a nun. At the age of twelve, she revealed that plan to an older sister. Her sister told her she'd better not tell anyone else because if she ever changed her mind, for the rest of her life people would look at her as a kind of nun-gone-bad. Lucy sealed her lips but not her heart. She was going to be a nun.

When she was a little older, she got an after-school job at Columbus Hospital. So did her friend Arlene Van Dusen. On their way to work they used to stop by the chapel of the hospital where Mother Cabrini had died in 1917. Lucy and Arlene even became blood Sisters, pressing their bleeding fingers together to form a lifelong bond. Then it turned out Arlene had a secret. She, too, wanted to be a nun.

As the two friends neared the end of high school, they decided it was time to turn their dream into reality. They skipped their senior prom and used the money to take a train to West Park, N.Y., where the Missionary Sisters of the Sacred

Walking on Sacred Ground

Heart had a novitiate. There the girls met other girls who shared the dream, students from Cabrini High School in New York. They talked. They shared. In a sense, this communal encounter was the beginning, just a baby step, of their formation as Sisters.

Lucy and Arlene went back to Chicago to give their parents the news and get their written permission to enter the convent. Arlene's grandmother took it well, as did Lucy's mother. Her father, however, was distraught. He put his foot down. "One is enough," he said, referring to the daughter they'd left in a convent back in Sicily. He would not be consoled; Lucy would not be deterred. She packed her suitcase in secret. Her mother supported the decision and got her husband to sign away permission for Lucy to join the MSCs. When the day came, Lucy and Arlene, in the black habits of postulants, boarded the train to New York. Their families were at the station. Everyone crying and wishing them good luck and a good life. At the time, entry into a religious congregation meant never seeing family again except at funerals. Lucy's family knew that the MSCs were doing missionary work in Australia. She and Lucy's father assumed, or at least feared, that's where their daughter would be going, to the other side of the world, never to return. Lucy later found out that when her parents got home, her father went to their bedroom alone, lay on the bed, and bawled his eyes out.

That was in 1966. Formation for religious life was different then. Postulants received just two weeks of training before being dispatched on an "experience," their first shot at missionary work. Lucy was assigned to teach at Cabrini Grammar School in New York City. With no more than two weeks of pedagogical preparation, she was given a class of second-graders. It was right next to the principal's office. The principal came into her class only once. The rest of the time just listened in through the wall.

The year went reasonably well. A roomful of eight-year-olds didn't dissuade Sister Lucy from religious life. Her experience a success, she returned to West Park. This was right after Vatican II called on congregations to get more serious in their training and their missions. Formation was intensified. Novices had a year to "discern" the implications of their future as Sisters. They had to take classes on the nature of their vows. They had to write papers on the charism of their founder, Mother Cabrini, the first American citizen to be canonized. They had to understand—at least begin to understand—the spirituality of the Sacred Heart of Jesus. Besides the classes for religious life, they took traditional classes in history and other academic subjects given by professors from Marist College in Hyde Park, New York. It was an intense education, a lot of work, though for Lucy, learning was a labor of love.

After a year, MSC novices were given the opportunity to extend their novitiate. Lucy and others opted for the second year. They saw that religious life, especially for missionary Sisters, wasn't as simple as they might have thought. They weren't going to take vows until they had enough formation.

"Formation has to be built on a rock, not on sand," Sister Lucy says today. "If you don't really have a sense of belonging to the congregation, if your personal charism doesn't fit in with the congregation's charism like a hand in a glove, you will not be able to live religious life."

After a year and ten months of preparation—all too quick by today's standards—Lucy and colleagues took their first vows. These first vows were canonically temporary. After three years, a Sister could change her mind. But spiritually or in the person's heart, those first vows are taken as if for life. The Sister can't be thinking, OK, I'll take the vows and see how it goes; I can always change my mind. No. She has to be thinking and truly believing that she is committing herself to the service of God for the rest of her days on earth.

Lucy so believed. Taking her vows, she became a sister in temporary vows. She would still be in the process of discernment, but she would now be addressed as Sister. She could move forward. She and her colleagues would go to Cabrini College, in Radnor, Pennsylvania, but Lucy wanted to study nursing, so she was given permission to transfer to Temple University, on the south and unsavory side of Philadelphia.

Four years later, in 1973, she graduated with a Bachelor of Science degree in Nursing. Her first assignment was to Cabrini Hospital in Seattle. It was a nice hospital, small, homey, and beautiful. The doctors were nice, and everyone knew everyone. Some 25 Sisters were living in the community, and the majority worked in the hospital. Sister Lucy was the youngest. She worked as scrub and circulating nurse on the surgery floor, then became nursing coordinator of the medical floor.

But then one day the nurses, the non-Sister nurses, went on strike. For the next three months, Sisters had to work 14 hours a day. Lucy had to care for 75 patients until the strike was settled.

Then it was time for her to consider perpetual vows. It was a big decision. After all due discernment and preparation, she took her vows at Cabrini Retreat Center in Des Plains, Illinois. Her whole family was there. It was beautiful.

Then it was back to Seattle to be a Community Superior, where again Sister Lucy was the youngest Sister around. General Superior Sister Regina Casey gave her another assignment, a tough one. She was going to have to get a degree in psychology. The congregation needed more Sisters in the mission of formation in the different countries where the MSCs were. The formation program had to better prepare young women for religious life. It would be based on personal work, on the understanding of the human person, and the need for sacrifice and transcendence. It is very difficult for a Sister to fully give herself to Jesus and His Kingdom in a Perpetual Commitment if she has a weak self.

Sister Lucy applied to the Gregorian University in Rome, where only fifteen students were selected from around the world. She got onto the waiting list and enrolled in the next year. It was a tough course, focusing on psychology with a specialization in the consecrated and ordained life. It was something the Missionary Sisters of the Sacred Heart of Jesus needed in the face of modern society. Candidates needed a lot of formation to gain a sense of belonging. They needed to adjust their lives and values in order to survive the turbulent social waters around them. The Institute needed to ensure that those who took vows were going to thrive in the very special life of a missionary Sister.

The course at Gregorian involved ongoing psychotherapy for each student. The belief was that one could not work with other people if one hadn't worked with one's self first. As Sister Lucy puts it, "If you don't face your own demons and your own conflicts, how can you help other people face theirs?" So each student met with a therapist twice a week. Lucy herself, though not by her assessment a terribly complicated person, had quite a few insights.

They also had to do clinical studies and observe other people under therapy. They also carried a full load of courses, with lectures in Italian and most readings in English. Already knowing these two languages, Lucy had it a lot easier than her peers from Italy, Brazil, Philippines, India, Germany, Ireland and the United States. It was hard, but a good hard. Sister Lucy remembers her time there as the best four years of her life. They prepared her for the next decades of hard work. She came away with a Licentiate in Psychology and everything she would have needed for a Ph.D., short of a thesis.

Where to go with a Licentiate in Psychology? A new General Superior, Suor Maria Barbagallo, gave her a couple of choices: Argentina or Central America. Another challenge for Sister Lucy—something else to learn! Spanish. She said yes to two months of discernment in Nicaragua and one month in

Guatemala.

This was in 1984, just after the Sandinista revolution and in the middle of the brutal, genocidal suppression in Guatemala. Next door, El Salvador was torn by a horrific civil war, and Honduras was barely keeping a lid on a simmering revolt. It was discernment in a crucible. The Sisters in Nicaragua were trying hard to get along with the socialist Sandinistas. The new government and the Congregation shared an intention to help the poor, but there was some friction between the church of the poor with Liberation Theology and the Hierarchical Church. There was also friction—violent friction—with the Contra counter-revolutionaries financed by the United States. Sister Lucy was very much supportive of the option for the poor and the parallel intentions of the Sandinista government, but she abhorred the national anthem when it sang of "Yankees" as enemies of humanity. She stood when the Sandinista's anthem was played, but she refused to sing it.

The Regional Superior, Hermana Juana Zoraida Mendoza, wanted Sister Lucy to have the "interior" experience, that is, an experience in a rural area outside the capital. She sent Sister Lucy to the harsh, impoverished village of Matiguás, where the Cabrini Sisters had an agricultural school. Hermana Matilde Giovagnoli, from Argentina, was the Superior there. When it came time to pick coffee, everyone was more or less required to volunteer to help. The Cabrini Sisters pitched in so Sister Lucy with a Sister companion went to a farm nearby to help pick coffee. On returning to the community in Matiguás, there was a report of imminent contra attack, Hermana Matilde Giovagnoli told Sister Lucy she had to leave the scene. Since she was an American, it was essential that she not be involved. She was hustled off in an ambulance to the nearby town of Matagalpa. A family there received her lovingly, and when it was time to sleep, they gave her a bedroom. From there, all night, she could hear the sickening sounds of the distant battle. In horror she thought of her Sisters there. That wasn't all that kept her awake. The room was crawling with mice. She stayed awake, sitting on her bed, writing in her journal and listening to the squeaking and scurrying, the gunfire and the explosions. The next morning she was put on a bus to Managua. Not yet understanding much Spanish, her imagination worked overtime. It was only four days later that Hermana Matilde showed up with the news. The coffee plantation where they had helped to pick coffee was completely destroyed, but the Sisters were unscathed.

That was enough discernment for Nicaragua. Off to Guatemala. The situation was tense and violent there, too. The violence was mostly in remote villages, but even in the capital, people often disappeared in the hands of the military. Sister Lucy was there a month, then went back to the United States, where she met with General Superior Maria Barbagallo. Suor Maria asked how the discernment had gone. Lucy said it didn't really matter how it had gone; she'd go wherever she was needed. So Suor Maria sent her back to Central America. She was to be directress of formation working out of the novitiate in Guatemala City. There were many women interested in religious life waiting to go through the process of discernment. Eventually only four young women became candidates at the house of formation in Guatemala. The others became good wives and mothers and an asset to their local church. There were more candidates in Argentina, so Central America and Argentina merged their initial formation, and it was decided to send them to the novitiate in Guatemala.

From her work one-on-one with the novices and juniors, Sister Lucy learned a lot. There's something hugely educational, she says, about going deeply into other people's lives. It's also, in a way, treacherous. Whenever she's inducing a young woman to speak about her past, her inner-most concerns, her most private spaces, her traumas and demons, Lucy remembers Moses approaching the burning bush, when God said "put off thy shoes from off thy feet, for the place whereon thou standest is sacred ground." That, she says, is what she does in the formation process. She treads ever so lightly. She looks to learn the strength that each person has, which gives her strength because she is trying to get that strength out of them. It gives her a sense of awe that God is working in them. With the help of God, she can help them see that their past is their past, their history, and they have to take it as their own, and it has to become their own history of salvation that has brought them to this beautiful period in their life.

At that point, after a regional discernment, Suor Maria asked Sister Lucy to take on the mission of Regional Superior while continuing as directress of the novitiate. It was a lot of work, but the Sisters in Nicaragua were very helpful, especially her secretary, Sister Gilda Mendoza. Sister Gilda was in charge of the agricultural school in Diriamba, Nicaragua, and agreed to be a counselor and secretary. Every month Sr. Lucy spent three weeks in Guatemala and one in Nicaragua and when necessary extended her stay in Nicaragua.

The trips back and forth between the countries, usually made by van, were fraught with danger. To avoid the conflict in El Salvador, they had to drive a longer route through Honduras. Border crossings were tense. The military governments associated religious workers with communist sympathizers because they worked with the poor. Sister Lucy remembers one time when she was sure her fate would be the same as that of Maryknoll Sisters Maura Clarke and Ita Ford, Ursuline Sister Dorothy Kazel, and the lay missionary with them, Jean Donovan. They were abducted, raped, and murdered by soldiers near the San Salvador airport. The same fate happened to Sister Diana Ortiz, an Urseline Sister who was abducted in 1989 in Guatemala, tortured and raped. Sister Diana was able to escape from her adductors to tell the story today and work for those who are abducted and tortured.

That was 1990 through 1991. The situation was still dangerous for religious men and women, and they were still struggling for social justice. The Missionary Sisters were commemorating the centenary of St. Frances Cabrini's arrival in Nicaragua in 1890. It was to be a year of centenary activities. Part of the event in Managua was an assembly to present the reality of the violence and injustices in Guatemala as well as Nicaragua. Sister Lucy's House of Formation was in charge of the presentation of the reality in Guatemala. The presentation included a slide show with images of people who had been tortured or killed. They had an opening Mass and reception in Granada where Mother Cabrini had begun her first school. As a matter of protocol, they invited government officials, including President Daniel Ortega. They never expected the president to show up, but he did, along with an entourage and bodyguards. From there, they were to go to a reception at a convent nearby. Two Sisters were to accompany President Ortega in his car. A newspaper photographed all the handshakes that preceded the ride, and the next day, the pictures were in the paper—MSCs shaking hands with a Sandinista. The Sisters didn't attach much importance to it at the time.

After the assembly, Sister Lucy and her candidates, Novices, and junior Sisters packed up for the drive back to Guatemala. Sister Lucy forgot to tell the Sisters to leave the "hard stuff"—the images and papers that attested to military abuses—with someone who would be going to Guatemala by plane. It would be safer. And off they went. But as they arrived at customs in Honduras, they found the place teeming with soldiers. Apparently the soldiers recognized the Sisters from the picture in the newspaper, all of them warm and friendly with a Sandinista. They asked the Sisters to give a policeman a ride to the border of Guatemala. Sister Lucy said No.

Then the soldiers proceeded to search the van. The Sisters

Walking on Sacred Ground

were very nervous. They worried that the soldiers might plant drugs or arms in the van, as they'd done with some Sisters of the Assumption a while before. Then Hermana Concepción Vallecillo whispered to Sister Lucy that the slide show was in her handbag. So was a book titled *Guatemala: Eternal Spring, Eternal Tyranny*, which detailed military abuses and injustices. So was an audio tape of the entire conference. It was enough to get them all thrown into prison...if they were lucky. They might well just disappear.

Sister Lucy was at the verge of panic. She didn't know what to do. So she turned to the Sacred Heart of Jesus and to Mother Cabrini. To the latter she whispered, "Mother, this is your mission I'm on. We are celebrating your centenary. You need to give me some strength here."

And it happened! Miraculously, Sister Lucy became calm and rational. While she took care of the passports for immigration, she asked for a volunteer to stay in the van. The Novice Mercedes Capdevielle, from Argentina, was the first to say "I will stay." The soldiers approached the van and pulled the Novice out of the van and began questioning her. Sister Lucy saw this from a distance and went over to the van, which was closed, despite soldiers searching around inside. She rolled the door open. An officer shut it. She rolled it open again. She said she had the right to see what was happening inside. His face burned with anger. As the Sisters looked in the windows, they saw a soldier find the slide show and the *Guatemala* book. The officer held a slide up to the sun. It was a propaganda picture of Guatemalan soldiers in front of a military base. The subtitle (translated) was "Guerilla Seen, Guerilla Killed." The officer demanded to know why they had such material. There were no words to explain. The soldiers confiscated various other suspicious materials. The Nicaraguan Sisters were really angry. They'd all lost family members or seen their families abused by the military forces of Anastasio Somoza. They knew what could happen. The officer ordered all the suitcases searched. Men climbed up on the roof of the van to open the suitcases. They poked around a bunch of books but didn't notice what they were about. After four or five hours, the women got their passports stamped, but the passports also got a secret mark that indicated a suspected subversive. The officer assigned a military escort to cross them through Honduras to the border with Guatemala. The escort kept the Nicaraguans' passport into his possessions the whole trip. The Sisters usually made a stop at Franciscan Convent half way in Honduras to rest for the night, leaving for Guatemala early the next day. The officer stayed in a room next to the garage where the Sisters had parked the van. At this point two Sisters told Sister Lucy that they had three books that were given to them that could be considered subversive. And they still had the audio tape in their possession. They went into the bathroom, cut the tape to pieces, and flushed them down the toilet. They buried the books in the back yard.

At two in the morning Hermana Concepción knocked on Sister Lucy's door, white as a ghost. She could not sleep, thinking that the soldiers might have planted drugs or arms in the van. Sister Lucy and Hermana Concepción, silent as mice, went to the van for a careful search for contraband and subversive material that could be used to accuse them at the next border. This had to be done in a way that the officer in the room to the side would not wake up and find them in the van. The Sisters did not find any evidence. After a tense drive across Honduras, they arrived in Guatemala. Soon thereafter they sold the van because it had been identified as belonging to communist sympathizers.

Some of the MSC's working in Guatemala went up into the mountains occasionally to visit remote villages. They took the Novices, Hermana Concepción Vallecillo, a medical doctor, and Sister Lucy as assistant nurse. They would see hundreds of patients in one day. As one Sister put it, "It looked like the crowd that was surrounding Jesus, waiting to be healed."

One time they arrived at a village after receiving a message that a young Protestant man was in critical condition and dying in his hut. The message said that an evangelical pastor was trying to convince the man's wife and the parents that death was inevitable and that they should have faith that God was waiting for his soul. The messenger, a Catholic indigenous friend, thought maybe the Sisters could do something to save him. The Sisters set off on foot, hiking over a mountain with their guide. They found the critical young man at the point of death. Hermana Concepción could not examine the patient because of the family's crying and screaming. But when she finally did, she found that he needed an emergency operation for bowel obstruction. She asked him if he wanted to live. In a very weak voice, the patient said Yes. The Sisters made a proposal to the parents and wife, that they would take him to the nearest hospital, which was in Santa Cruz. The sisters didn't know how to get him there, but they had to try. There was no way of getting the van to the hut. Quickly it was decided they would build a make-shift stretcher and bring him down to a point on the mountain where Sister Lucy could reach him with a four wheel drive van. Men carried the patient to the meeting place. At the hospital, the man was quickly prepared for surgery. The Sisters had to look for an open pharmacy to buy a list of things that the hospital required for the operation, even the necessary sutures. Of course the man's wife had no money, but the Sisters were able to buy what was necessary. The Sisters then left to go back to their mission. They had to pass various check points that were posted to look for rebel soldiers. It was a very frightening experience, but the Sacred Heart of Jesus and Mother Cabrini were with them. Six months later, Sister Lucy was approached by a very tall handsome man in the mission. He asked her "Are you Sister Lucy?" He then thanked all the Sisters for saving his life.

Events like this were some of the consolations for the Sisters in these very dangerous missions. They often had to backpack medicines into places with no roads. At times the food was exquisite. Sometimes it was hard to swallow. Sometimes they had to flick flies out of their soup. The strength came from their love for the mission. Sometimes the Sisters got sick. Once Sister

Walking on Sacred Ground

Lucy got a nasty parasite, giardia, apparently from just a sip of untreated water. The rather messy symptoms were made no easier by a latrine half a mile away. Once back in the capital, she was on intravenous medication for ten days.

That went on for ten years. Then Sister Lucy was sent to Argentina. She spent the first year as directress of Novices, and then a year as Provincial Superior. After the first year, all the Novices took their vows, and Lucy could dedicate her time to the Province. A new mission was opened in Sierra Grande among the poor of Patagonia. Sister Lucy made many 18-hour bus trips to visit the Sisters and share with them.

* * *

After being Provincial in Argentina for six years, Sister Lucy was missioned back to Central America to the grammar school at Ducuali in Managua. This community was to be the House of Formation for candidates for Religious life. Here again she prepared young women for the novitiate. At that time the novitiate was in Italy and later in Brazil.

While Sister Lucy was Regional Superior, the MSCs opened a community in Altar, Mexico, near the border with Arizona. The house was staffed by three pioneer Sisters: Hermana Juana Mendoza Sandino, Hermana Carmen Pantano and Hermana Beatriz Caal. In classic Cabrini charism, the mission at Altar is dedicated to helping migrants. The Sisters first try to indirectly talk people out of attempting to cross the border. They

213

describe the dangers of thirst, heat stroke, dishonest coyotes, rattlesnakes, thorns, and all the hazards of hiking quickly in the dark. If anyone wants to go back home, the Sisters help. It would probably be the wiser choice, but most have already abandoned their old lives, spent every bit of their pitiful savings plus whatever they could borrow. Going back home is not an option.

Sister Lucy was there when four young Mexican migrants arrived—a young woman, two younger brothers, and their cousin. They set out with a coyote and spent the first night out in the desert somewhere. Of course they had no idea where they were. The next day, on the U.S. side of the border but still way out in the desert, the girl hurt her ankle so bad she couldn't walk. It looked broken. There wasn't much anyone could do about it. They couldn't carry her, and they couldn't slow down or they'd all die. They had to leave her. She told her brothers and cousin to go ahead, but the brothers weren't going to abandon their sister. The cousin went ahead. The brothers helped her hobble back into Mexican territory, where they called someone on their cell phone. A woman answered. It was a wrong number. But the woman was kind enough to call the right number. The parish priest, Padre Prisciliano, went out to pick them up. He does this often, makes a regular patrol to look for people who are stranded or dead.

Sister Lucy continued her work in Central America from 2001 to 2010. Then she was given a chance to rest in silence, prayer and contemplation at the Desert House of Prayer in

Walking on Sacred Ground

Arizona. She was given approval to visit the Holy Land for ten days. And then she was sent to Ethiopia.

At an oasis in the harsh, dry backlands of that country, the MSCs have a House of Formation and center for poor and orphaned children. The Sisters also operate a hospital for the local diocese. For the children they have several programs. The Sisters run various pre-school programs. In the summer, when the pre-school is closed, the children can come and get a meal. Parents are expected to do a bit of work, for pay, at the Center two days a week for two hours so that their children have free pre-school, clothing, and food, and the parents have some spending money to provide for their children. There are also training programs for parents. Mothers can come learn to spin cotton into shawls. A youth group, the Francescinas (Little Franciscans, named after Madre Francesca Xavier Cabrini), teaches kids hygiene, skills, morals, and catechism. Water is a little scarce in the area, so the Sisters had a well dug and plumbing laid out so people can come bathe and wash clothes and get clean water for their households. With donations from other countries, the Center has been able to buy cows and chickens so people have fresh milk and eggs. There was also funding for a bakery, so that the hospital and the Sisters with the candidates and novices have fresh bread. The Center used to take in abandoned babies, some of whom had been literally abandoned on the Center doorstep. But there were problems with the administration, and eventually the orphanage closed.

Sister Lucy's job was what she does best—formation.

This is a special challenge in Ethiopia. For one thing, over 82 languages are spoken in that country. If aspirants don't know Amharic, they have to learn it, and eventually they must learn English as well. To become an aspirant, they need to have completed secondary school, which can be difficult in such an impoverished nation. The MSCs prepare each woman with further studies even if there's little chance they will go on to become Sisters. The object is to prepare young women for life.

One big challenge is to perceive which young women really have the vocation for religious life. This takes years, but all the teaching, training, praying, and formation are beneficial even for young women who are directed into a secular profession. For every educated woman, the world is better off.

Most people in Ethiopia are Christian orthodox. A small percentage are Catholics, and there are assorted Protestant churches. Muslims are second in number in the country. Religious roots go back to the cradle of Judeo-Christianity. The Queen of Sheba is believed to have been Ethiopian. So there are many young women wishing to opt for the religious life. But they need much education, much discernment, and much formation. Sister Lucy was very busy with various tasks helping Suor Therese Merandi and Suor Regina Canale.

Sister Lucy also got very sick. After her years in Central America, she was used to being sick with parasites and dengue, but in Ethiopia she got typhoid several times and malaria twice. The second bout with malaria and typhoid was really bad. The General Superior had to pull her out of Ethiopia before she reached critical condition. Sister Lucy didn't want to go. There was so much to do, so many young women in the process of formation, so many children, so much potential. She had nine Sisters in temporary vows, and three to become candidates, and another thirty or so at different stages of preparation. When she left, she felt she was abandoning them all, especially the new Sisters and Sisters Therese, Francesca and Sister Regina.

But she felt God's hand in the move. The Cabrini Sisters' mission in West Park, N.Y., on a hill overlooking the Hudson, was being established as an international house of formation for MSC Novices and young women from all over the world who have not yet taken perpetual vows. Sister Lucy is the directress. It's a perfect place for her, a perfect mission. Right back where she started from as a Novice. But she's back with baggage. She's been around and seen a lot. When young women begin their formation journey, she knows something about where they're coming from, and she knows how to walk on their sacred ground. She helps them strengthen their relationship with Jesus so they can work tirelessly for His people. She does it all for the greater glory of the Sacred Heart of Jesus and with the charism of St. Paul and Mother Cabrini: "I can do all in Christ who strengthens me."

Swaziland

Love and Death

Once upon a time in the Kingdom of Swaziland, life was as good as it was going to get. The folk in the country lived in little round houses of mud, sticks, and reeds. They planted gardens and let their cattle wander around. The folk in the city found jobs, ate imported food, drove imported cars on paved highways. On Sundays, they went to church. They laughed a lot. They drank the tap water. In February, everybody got drunk on home-brewed murula fruit hootch. In the rainy season, it rained. In August, everybody watched bare-breasted maidens perform the annual reed dance. The king would be there, perhaps to pick another wife. The Swazi culture, millennia old, kept everyone knitted together in a handful of vast families. Orphans were genealogically impossible.

They had their unspeakable side: black magic, witch

doctors, social paranoia, chattel-women, abominable sacrifices. They used the same word for love, like, fornicate, and rape. But this culture, dark and bizarre by the standards of the white world, somehow worked to sustain them in a place of thorn bushes, pit vipers, and wars fought with spears and knobkierrie clubs. Seventy percent of the population was rural, and the level of ignorance wasn't advanced much beyond the dark ages. Illiteracy outside a couple of cities was general, beliefs almost prehistoric. Though Protestant and Catholic churches claimed over 80 percent of the population, age-old beliefs ran deep beneath the veneer of Christianity.

For many years Swaziland benefited from the racial nastiness of the neighbor that bordered the kingdom on three sides. When the world refused to do business with the South African apartheid regime, companies from that country set up camp in the little kingdom four hours east of Johannesburg. Though the country was landlocked and without a train line through South Africa or Mozambique to the coast, the economy boomed. King Sobhuza II reaped plenty of revenues and used them not only to take good care of himself, his 70 wives, and his 210 children, but to pass out food, sponsor clinics, support schools, fill potholes, and keep cities livable. He worked with the chiefs of chiefdoms to keep people happy. When he dispensed with the constitution the British colonizers had imposed, no one cared. Everyone loved King Sobhuza.

Sobhuza died in 1982, but his successor, one of many sons, was only 14 years old. Two queen mothers ran the country in succession until the boy turned 18. He was in high school in England when they called him back to be groomed for the throne. In 1986, a week after his eighteenth birthday, he became King Mswati III.

Mswati didn't have much time to learn to be a king. In 1992, drought descended on Swaziland. In 1994, apartheid collapsed, the international boycotts stopped, and the South African companies went home. And then everybody started dying.

That was what Irmã Ana Maria de Oliveira said on the phone to her Province Superior, Sister Diane DalleMolle, when she heard that the Cabrini Sisters, were retracting her mission from Swaziland. Everybody was dying.

"We can't leave now," she pleaded. "Everybody's dying. Everybody." And she started crying. All the babies she and Suor Speranza D'Ambrosi had delivered, educated, raised to adulthood, and trained for a job were all dying. The work of three decades, a whole generation of people, a little impulse of hope for the struggling kingdom, was wasting away.

Irmã Ana Maria said, "All we can do is go out to the homesteads and bring them some food and sit with them while they die. Children are everywhere. What are we going to do with all the children?"

Sister Diane had no idea what to do with the children. She was overseeing missions in several countries, from the United States to Australia to Taiwan. That was in 1997. Average life expectancy in Swaziland had already declined from sixty-something to 56, and projections were tilting down at a Titanic angle. The Missionary Sisters of the Sacred Heart had been in Swaziland for 30 years, maintaining a school and convent near Manzini, Swaziland's largest city, and a clinic in the harsh, dusty outback of the Lubombo district, a parish-based outpost called St. Philip's. Things had been going so well in the country that the Sisters no longer felt needed. The world had more desperate places.

But then Sister Diane got a call from her General Superior in Rome. She'd heard of the decision to pull out. She said to Diane, "Don't do it."

And Diane asked, "Why not?"

And the General Superior said, "Just don't."

She had grabbed Diane's heart, but her managerial brain needed a reason.

"I can't give you a reason. We just need to stay if we are ever to do the work that God wants us to do. We have to stay in places that seem impossible."

Sister Diane went to see the situation. She flew into Johannesburg, then took a little plane into Swaziland, then took a car an hour down paved roads, then an hour down a bumpy dirt road. She found St. Philip's above the west bank of the Mhlatuze River, which, in the ongoing drought, often barely qualified as a creek. The mission consisted of a few low buildings that housed a little clinic, some staff, the parish priest, an elementary school, and a high school. The church was a dome supported by concrete arches, built, it would seem, to

222

Love and Death

echo sweet Swazi hymns.

And there she found just about everyone dying. Irmã Ana Maria took her to some homesteads out among the thorn bushes. The average homestead was a small, circular, wattle-and-daub house with a reed roof. A fence of stick, stones, and thorny branches might surround the place. A few head of cattle and goats might be wandering around the scrub. A scarred and skinny dog might be sleeping in the dust. A few gristly chickens might be scratching around in search of infinitesimal bits of something edible. The houses had little or no furniture or even room for furniture. Rare was the house without at least one person slowly dying on a reed mat on the dirt floor. At one they found three girls lying on mats outside the house. They were sixteen, seventeen, and eighteen years old, all in the fourth and last stage of AIDS, all infected by the same man. One girl's uterus was distended from her body and covered with fungus. All three had fungal growths around their mouths and down their throats. Their mother was trying to care for them, but there was little she could do.

Cabrini's little clinic didn't have the technical capability to diagnose what Ana Maria and Speranza knew to be the problem. Even if they could, they had no way to treat HIV/AIDS. Every day more leathery black skeletons staggered in on their spindly knobkierrie staffs. But treatment was superficial at best. The best the Sisters could do was alleviate some of the symptoms. The people had to drag themselves back home to die.

And it was time for the Sisters to go home, too. Ana Maria

was 75, Speranza 85.

Diane wasn't one to walk away from dying people. She had to go back to New York to plead for Swaziland, but something tied her to St. Philip's. As she boarded the little plane to Johannesburg, she was still covered with grit. It was even in her teeth. When she pulled her shoes off to shake them clean, she realized that she loved even the dust of that place.

Back in New York she became more conscious of the oppressive enormity of her job as Provincial Superior. Though a nurse by training, she was overseeing 20 hospitals, clinics, and other institutions. Her congregation's hospital in New York—1,100 beds, 500 employees— was struggling in the industry's maelstrom of regulations, law suits, restructuring, union demands, technology, AIDS, and soaring costs amid widening poverty. She was spending more in a month than the mission in Swaziland could spend in 20 years. She wanted out, and the outback of Swaziland was about as far out as a Cabrini Sister could get. She wanted to go there, she said, to save her everlasting soul. Her work in New York was God's work, she knew, but it felt like she was walking the other way.

Her board approved an extension of the mission. Ana Maria would go back to her native Brazil, Speranza to New York. Diane would replace them, downshifting, she thought, into a simpler life. She was 61. That was in 2004. Life expectancy in Swaziland had declined to 37 and was still dropping.

But Swaziland wasn't so simple. Instead of lawyers, bankers, union officials, consultants, administrators, and

Love and Death

government regulators, she faced plague, drought, corruption, decimated families, legions of orphans, endemic rape, black magic, and ignorance rooted in an impenetrable culture. The government, medieval in its structure and its disregard for its people, obstructed change to any status quo and showed no concern for the well-being of citizens. Dr. Henk Bos had been at St. Philip's for a couple of years. He was the director of laboratories at the Cabrini hospital in Australia. As he handed the mission to Sister Diane, he offered no words of optimism, no illusions of a problem solved or solvable. He told her she would never be able do what she'd come to do, that the problem was impossible to solve. She didn't know what she was doing, didn't know what she'd gotten into. Then he got into the little plane to Johannesburg and flew away.

Diane had second thoughts. They pursued her into bed that night. Lying in the dark of that strange and scary land, she realized that Dr. Henk didn't understand who the daughters of Mother Cabrini were, that they had always done what they didn't know how to do, that they didn't surrender to impossibility, not when people were standing in front of them dying.

That disregard for impossibility had always been the history and mission of the MSCs. Mother Cabrini had never let impossibility stand in her way. Dynamic and unstoppable, she founded and secured funding for schools, hospitals, and orphanages in the United States, Nicaragua, Argentina, Brazil, and Europe—all quite impossible for a woman at that period in history, yet she was able to accomplish it. She was canonized in 1946.

Before they retired from St. Philip's, Sisters Ana Maria and Speranza put their hands and compassion together to pull off one more impossibility. They managed to get an orphanage built for fifty children. More precisely defined, it was a hostel, a place where children could stay most of the year. During school breaks they would go back to whoever had last been taking care of them. On the day the hostel opened, 98 children showed up. The Sisters put them two to a bed. More showed up the next day. It was a lot of kids to feed, love, and clean up after. The local staff needed a lot of training in the art of raising children. For one thing, they had to learn that beating traumatized children is not the best way to discipline them.

Diane, too, had a lot to learn. She was the only white woman in an area raging with a worsening epidemic. She had one small health clinic staffed with a few Swazi nurses, and she had a hostel with well over a hundred children. She awoke every morning to find people dying on her porch. It was a lot for one woman to handle. She called her Provincial Superior in New York and asked if Sister Barbara Staley could be assigned to Swaziland. Barbara had a master's degree in social work and had done time in the jungles of Guatemala and the slums of Chicago. She knew how to work with children. She knew how to plan. She knew how to not just get things done but make them get done.

The Province Superior said No. Diane pleaded with all her heart. Then she made a bargain she'd never be able to keep. She said she needed Barbara for just three months. She knew perfectly well she was going to keep finding reasons why Barbara couldn't leave. Barbara arrived in late 2004.

Barbara knew how to devise a plan and then execute it, but there was little point in planning anything. As soon as she got off the little plane, she was dealing with immediate problems—the people dying on the porch, the venomous black mamba coiled up in a tree in the back yard, the dilapidated homestead headed by an unprotected prepubescent girl, the car stuck in the river. These problems didn't need plans. They needed immediate attention. Every day, starting well before dawn, Sister Barbara and Sister Diane had to confront the life-and-death urgency of right now.

And they didn't know what they were doing. They had never confronted an epidemic before and certainly had no idea how to treat HIV infection or AIDS. They had no one to advise them on anything. They had no idea how the medical system worked in Swaziland, no idea where to buy food for a hundred-odd children every day, how to train illiterate people, how to run a clinic staffed with nurses who believed black magic worked. They had no time to learn siSwati.

As they started to establish initial measures for dealing with the epidemic, they hit their first inexplicable wall. Everyone was deathly ill, and in most cases it was pretty obvious what the cause was. Step one toward treatment was to have blood tested, yet people were refusing. In fact, the people working with Diane and Barbara refused to even ask people to be tested. Not even nurses would do it. But it made no sense. Though the causes of HIV, from rape to polygamy, held no stigma, having the disease was embarrassing, and asking about it was insulting. The Sisters hired a local leader, Mr. Pius Mamba, to provide the language and cultural insight they needed to talk with people. He'd been raised in the rural culture, but he'd always been a Christian and had quite a bit of college education. He went out to the homesteads with the Sisters to translate, but he, too, had difficulty asking about testing for HIV. He had to gradually, over the course of half an hour, lead into the question. "Forgive me for being so bold," he'd say. "It isn't me asking this, it's the Sister; she's white, you know...a little crazy; I'm just translating and I need this job, so I have to ask, if you could just try to understand that I don't mean anything by it..." And then all he could do was hope the question didn't lead to a curse that only a witch doctor could remove.

Oddly enough, once the question was asked, the answer was often a desperate yes. So in dark, smoke-filled huts, Diane drew blood. Because of the dim light, the tough muscle tissue of dirt farmers, the dark skin over collapsed veins, she had to use her bare fingers to find a vein and guide the needle in. Then she'd put the blood on ice to take to Good Shepherd Hospital for testing. Sometimes the blood spent the night in plastic bags in the refrigerator back home, in there with the food. It was the only refrigerator they had.

When the test for HIV came back positive, they would have to take the patient to the hospital. They'd be rumbling down

Love and Death

unmapped dirt trails by 4:00 a.m. It was the only way to have enough time to pick up Mr. Mamba, find far-flung homesteads, talk people into allowing a blood draw, pick up patients, go to the hospital two hours to the northeast, take blood samples into Manzini for HIV testing, take other samples into the capital, Mbabane, for CD4 testing of white blood cell levels, and then go back to homesteads to inform those who had to go to the hospital the next morning. They packed as many people as they could into an old Toyota Venture, a mini-van modified to hold more passengers than it was built for. It had problems. It was a four-wheel drive vehicle, but only two wheels drove. The battery kept falling out. The lights kept going off. The tires kept going flat. A wheel kept coming off. Not built for off-road travel, the van tended to get stuck in rivers they were driving through, in soft sand, in puddles of dust. On the way to the hospital one night, just after repairs to the electrical system, the lights went out and flames licked out from under the hood. Diane couldn't stop for that. She held a flashlight out the window in case other cars couldn't see the flames coming down the road.

    She was a nurse, not a mechanic, and she was at the wheel of a logistical nightmare. She wasn't even much of a driver, either. She didn't know how to drive a standard shift until she got to Swaziland. She didn't know what to do with a battery hanging under the engine, swaying by a cable. She didn't know how to change a flat until Mr. Mamba, who is blind, talked her through it one dark night. She learned to keep a flashlight in the car.

Good Shepherd wasn't much of a hospital. It certainly wasn't up to the challenge of an AIDS epidemic. HIV patients were laid out on the floor of a space not much bigger than a living room. A couple hundred more lay on the ground outside. The only doctor, an American from California, was always angry and shouting, way over his head in patients, dealing with inadequate staff, dispensing inadequate medications, and working with inadequate equipment.

To simply leave patients at Good Shepherd wouldn't be much better than leaving them at home. They were as ignorant as could be, as humble as dirt, unable to understand instructions, afraid to speak up, mystified by the whole medical process. The Sisters had to speak for, and think for, their patients. Mr. Mamba said to Sister Barbara, "You care more about these people's lives than they do."

The conditions at homesteads had declined from third-world to sub-human. The Sisters came to homesteads so poor that people were walking around naked. They found young children trying to maintain a household while a tubercular parent in the fourth stage of AIDS lay fetid and suppurating on the floor in a cluster of jubilant flies. Water had to come from a river a mile or two or more away, and if the river was dry at that time of year, they'd have to dig. Due to the drought, no one had harvested a crop in a decade. Due to lack of people healthy enough to work, houses were falling apart, mud walls eroding, reed roofs disintegrating. As parents died, children got passed to aunts and uncles until they died, then to grandmothers

Love and Death

until they died, then to neighbors, then to the grandmothers of neighbors. Children lost track of where they were born and who their parents were. Some lost track of their own names. As they distanced themselves from their families and homesteads, they lost their inheritance of family homesteads. Old women found themselves with herds of children from unknown places, everyone sleeping on the floors of their little houses, sharing smoky air with people coughing up blood. No one in the world offered any help except the two old white women in the old Toyota, and they were lucky if they made it to half a dozen homesteads in a day, half a dozen out of 2,500 around St. Philip's.

At one homestead, apparently abandoned after the roof fell in, they looked around, found nobody. They asked a neighbor who said there was a small baby being cared for at the house by a "troubled" young girl and an old man. The Sisters went back to the house, poked around, found a rib-skinny dog crouched beside a pile of rags. In the pile of rags they found a rib-skinny little boy named Menze. They picked him up. He didn't stir. He wasn't quite dead, but almost. The dog could have told them that. It was just waiting. The Sisters took him back to the mission and nursed him back into life.

These people weren't just patients. Barbara and Diane developed close relationships with many of them. When they died, they were friends dying—hundreds and hundreds of friends. The Sisters didn't cry much, but once in a while it happened. It happened to Diane the first time she got out of Swaziland. It was in 2006, after two years in-country. She went to a retreat in upstate New York, a place for prayer and contemplation. On the second day she got to contemplating about all the friends she'd seen die. She started sobbing and couldn't stop. She just sobbed and sobbed and sobbed.

Barbara sobbed when a girl named Tanzele died. Both of her parents had died, and she had HIV and tuberculosis. Twice a week she had to walk 19 kilometers to a clinic for medication. She was 13 when the Sisters took her into the hostel. In the magical way of Swazis, she became happy. Everyone loved her. She took her medications and went to school every day. She giggled with the other girls. She played a game that involved dodging a ball of wadded-up plastic bags while trying to fill a soda bottle with sand. She was so proud of her excellent report card. When she went home to stay with relatives during a school break, she contracted measles. Medical personnel and foreign aid workers didn't know what to do. They'd never seen anyone with HIV, TB, and measles. Barbara thought they didn't try hard enough to help her. When she died, Barbara wept—not just for the loss but for the fact of no one being able to save her. She wept for that and the reality that success had to be measured in such small increments. In Tanzele's case, it was a girl who was allowed to experience childhood for a few months.

There was hardly a day when either Diane or Barbara didn't decide to give up, to go home, to take on some other problem, one that could actually be solved. Every day was one day too much. But when they had time to stop and think about what they were doing, to relate their travails to Jesus, and to dispense with the notion of impossibility, they always managed to stay a little longer and go out to a few more homesteads to see what they could do. It's hard to walk away from people who are dying. In the dark of that strange and scary land, she realized that Dr. Henk didn't understand who the Missionary Sisters of the Sacred Heart were and what they were capable of.

People on the homesteads had no idea what was causing their maladies, which in a single individual were likely to include several sexually transmitted diseases. They might have tuberculosis that had spread from lungs to glands to bones. They often had Kaposi's sarcoma, a systemic viral infection that causes lesions on the skin, from soles to gums, down the gastrointestinal tract and into the lungs. They might have tumors under the arm, on the tongue, in the throat. They might have shingles as ugly and painful as a third-degree burn. They might have fungal growths down through the alimentary canal. They surely had chronic diarrhea. They had skin diseases Diane had never seen before. They had peripheral neuritis, an agonizing inflammation of the nerves of the lower leg. People in their twenties hobbled around like crippled elderly trying to keep their infected feet off the ground. Paranoid by the nature of their culture, they readily supposed they were the victims of a curse targeted at them as individuals. They didn't know how the disease spread, and when told, they didn't believe it. They believed what the "traditional healers" told them—that they had been cursed by a neighbor, that if the patient was a man, the prescribed cure might be sex with a virgin, or if the patient was a woman, the cure might be sex with the doctor himself. It might also involve little hash marks cut into the knuckles and other joints with a razor used on other people with the same medical complaint. Sometimes the healers, protective of their turf, told people to refuse the white medicine, that it would kill them.

The Sisters recognized that they had to work within this culture. But they found it unfathomable. No one, not even the people they worked with, not even the ones with education and urban experience, was willing to offer more than a peek into its dark secrets. Ever since the English and Dutch colonization of the 19th century Swazis had learned to keep their African side veiled. The national motto, Siyinqaba, could be translated as "We are a fortress" but with the parallel meaning of "We are hidden; we are a mystery."

They spoke English with foreigners in a beautiful, off-kilter, almost poetic whisper, but they rarely said more than necessary. They answered open-ended questions with vague thoughts that seemed framed to tell the white people only what they wanted to hear. They answered yes-no questions honestly but with just one word. They were polite to the point of self-effacing humility. Women were reluctant to speak with men and afraid to speak with whites. When women came into the Cabrini clinic, they could not bring themselves to look at Diane. They stood half bowed, half turned away, speaking in a timid hush. The treatment and prevention of HIV had to begin with basic education: getting women to stand straight and speak up, and not just to talk with Diane. They would have to stand straight and speak up to their doctors, their husbands, their chiefs, their sorceresses and witch doctors. But they were as comfortable doing this as American women would be singing operatic-style to all the men in their lives.

Behavior was inexplicable. People would get sick and frightened enough to come in for testing, but when they went home, they hit family problems. Their husbands wouldn't allow them to get treated. Or their sisters talked them out of it. Or their healers would offer a more traditional option. Or their preachers would tell them Jesus would heal them. One patient came in and said that her preacher had cured her. When he prayed over her, she could feel the moment she was healed. She didn't come back until she was almost dead. There was a staff member whose mother was a sorceress. He was a "default tracker" who excelled at going out into the outback to track down people who had stopped picking up medications. For three years he showed the symptoms of AIDS, but his mother refused to let him get tested. He died at the age of 35. They found him lying naked in a building, waiting for his spirit to return to his body. Then he couldn't be buried on his homestead because it was feared that the neighbors who had bewitched him with HIV would come dig up his bones to use for rituals.

As they grappled with the causes and prevention of HIV and orphanhood, they came to see how the culture itself was the crux of the problem. Women, especially those in rural areas, had no way to say no to sex. It didn't matter if the man was an uncle or someone else's husband or a stranger who happened to come along. It didn't matter if he was HIV-positive. Swazi culture instilled such submission in women that psychologically they could not bring themselves to resist sex. A girl might well be pushed into marriage as a young teen, especially if deflowered. Her father would be compensated for the loss by a payment of cattle. Depending on the girl's beauty, virtues, family connections, and extent of virginity, she could be worth ten or twenty cows, maybe more, maybe less. Her proposing groom would actually negotiate with her father, giving reasons why she wasn't worth as many cows as her father liked to think.

While women were submissive in sex, men were sexually unencumbered. Though a neighbor's wife was technically off limits, adultery was a matter of what one could get away with more than an issue of morality. An unmarried sister-in-law was fair game. Virginity was something to respect, but not out of concern for the girl. Rather, it was a matter of how many cows she was worth before and after. Once violated, she was obliged to marry. If the man already had a wife, well, now he had another, though it might cost him a few cows. The wives slept on the floor near their husband's bed. When he wanted to lie with one of them, he called her over. They had a special verb for that.

On the other hand, none of that is necessarily true. Swazi sexual mores are confusing, convoluted, and contradictory. Any non-Swazi claiming to understand it probably hasn't asked

Love and Death

enough Swazis to explain it. Barbara and Diane certainly didn't understand it.

Alcohol aggravated the situation. Home-based bars, called shebeens, sold a cheap, sweet, creamy home-made hootch made from the murula fruit. The fruit ripened in February. Everybody spent the next month or two drunk. Crime rose. Pregnancies increased. Disease spread. Dedicated alcoholics kept it up for the rest of the year. They hung around the shebeen all day, often leaving kids unattended at home. If the individual had TB, the close and palsy-walsy quarters of the shebeen facilitated its transmission. As the day's drinking built up, the benefits of condom usage got forgotten. Inebriation enhanced the beauty of the famished barflies, and desperation for another drink increased the acceptability of a man with money. If the individual was HIV-positive, which he or she probably was, the virus soon found its way into a nice, new bloodstream. And everybody took home some TB bacilli for the kids.

Pius Mamba, one of few willing to give the Sisters a little insight into Swazi culture, defined sex as a matter of power exchanged for pleasure. Women lacked social and economic power and privilege—the privilege of sitting on a chair rather than on the ground, of learning a trade and earning their own bread, of owning land, of deciding whom they would marry and how many children they would have and whom their husbands would marry. Their power was pretty much limited to how easily they would provide the pleasure of sex. Mr. Mamba called it "transactional sex." Women gave sex to get something, be it food, a cell phone, a ride into town, or a withholding of violence. While psychologically they couldn't say no, they could set some conditions for yes. They could try to get what they could for what they had to do anyway. Though other Swazis weren't necessarily as cynical (or articulate) as Mr. Mamba, his explanation was credible. Sister Diane knew a woman who was having sex with a man she knew to be HIV-positive. Her justification: "I'd rather die later with a full stomach than die hungry now."

Culture was at the root of the problem, but Barbara and Diane hadn't come to Swaziland to cure culture. They weren't even there to push Catholicism. Not exactly, not that directly. Yes, they believed the world was better off where Catholicism and its values were a way of life; yes, they would like to see more of it in Swaziland; no, they were not pushing it on people. They did not engage in catechism. Their mission was health care and child care. Yes, they led their children in Catholic prayer and Catholic song. Yes, they took their children to mass every Sunday. But aside from religious guidance for the children in the hostel, the Sisters were bringing the love of Jesus to the local people not by thumping a Bible but by providing example. As Diane put it, they were in circumstances where they were better off living the love of God than talking about it. They were teaching by doing, nurturing love by loving.

But the frustration of working with an incorrigible and uncooperative culture gave rise to anger. Sisters aren't supposed to experience anger, and they certainly aren't supposed to show it, but it happened. Like all Sisters and nuns who struggle with the world's intractable problems, Barbara and Diane have a certain fire in them. Without that fire, they wouldn't be able to do what they do. They probably wouldn't even try. It's a good fire, but like all fire, it can burn. There were times when they lost control and lashed out at somebody too stupid or sluggish to see what needed to be done. The negative impression left by these incidents would haunt them for years.

And they lashed out at each other, an inevitability when two people are exhausted and trying to solve problems which neither have seen before and which have no obvious solutions. But they were brief arguments free of ego or suspicion. They were both trying to accomplish the same thing, and they never had time for a drawn-out debate. They also understood the inevitability of failures along the way. Though a good deal of the time they didn't know what they were doing, at least they were doing something. Their failures were no worse than the default situation.

Toward the end of 2004, just months after the Sisters arrived in Swaziland, the first free anti-retrovirals (ARVs) came into the country courtesy of the Global Fund to Fight AIDS, Tuberculosis and Malaria. At the same time, the President's Emergency Plan for AIDS Relief (PEPFAR), initiated by George W. Bush, started providing financial and technical assistance for promoting capacity, competence, and sustainability. The Global Fund was funded by donations from governments, the private sector, philanthropic organizations and individuals. The Bill and Melinda Gates Foundation was the largest nongovernmental donor. The Global Fund provided (and carefully monitored) grants to governments to pay for medications and other materials.

In their first years dealing with the epidemic, the Sisters could offer nothing more than access to health care—the blood tests, the rides to the hospital, the education. Columbia University's International Center for AIDS Care and Treatment Programs (ICAP) came to St. Philip's to help raise the capacity of their local organization, Cabrini Ministries. Cabrini turned over its general clinic to the Severite Sisters, a diocesan order located at St. Philip's. On the next day, Cabrini opened a clinic dedicated to HIV/AIDS and TB. Big mistake. Because it was a new clinic, it had to go through all the government certification procedures again. But in time, as they increased their capacity, they would be able to test for HIV and TB and initiate treatments, avoiding the trips to Good Shepherd.

Anti-retrovirals, it turned out, worked better than sex with virgins and witch doctors. They didn't cure, but if combined with good nutrition, and if other illnesses were dealt with, ARVs could support immune systems enough for them to avoid the diseases associated with AIDS, prolonging life for more than a decade. They drastically reduced transmission of the virus through sex, and they could prevent contagion of newborns by their HIV-positive mothers.

In 2007, after knocking on innumerable doors and filing innumerable forms and beseeching innumerable government ministers and other officials, quite innocently neglecting to bribe

Love and Death

everyone along the way, they got Cabrini Ministries registered as a not-for-profit. Around about that time, they gained a reputation for not only getting things done but implementing new programs quickly. They had no organizational bureaucracy holding them back, and they were far enough out in the sticks to be overlooked by the government. They became a model for how to most efficiently and effectively implement new projects. Ironically, they were still flying by the seat of their calf-length skirts, figuring things out as they charged forward, finding solutions for impossible problems and moving on.

By this point, average life expectancy in Swaziland was edging down toward 32 years, probably lower in the Lubombo region. The national population was declining, something that had rarely happened anywhere on earth since the bubonic plague hit Europe in the 14th century.

Though working in a place dense with disease, the Sisters themselves had no time to be sick. They had to be in a lot of places at the same time. Mbabane was in the northwest corner of the country. Good Shepherd hospital was in Siteki, in the northeast corner of the country. Manzini was in the center of the country. St. Philip's was in the southeast. They had to move patients, medications, and blood samples to most of these places almost every day. They had to buy food in Manzini for the homesteads because the medications certainly weren't going to work on people who were starving. They had to divvy the food up into packages for delivery. They had to keep track of who had to go back to the hospital, who had children not being taken care of, who was failing to take their medications.

In the middle of all this, they were raising over a hundred traumatized children who needed a consistent supply of food, clothes, showers, and school materials. They needed warm words of encouragement in a cold, discouraging world. They needed admonishments for the gaffes and misdemeanors of childhood. They needed someone to explain the facts of life to them, including the fact that sex was synonymous with death. Their hostel needed a poster depicting a young, happy, hip-looking black woman saying, "I can live without sex."

The Sisters had to teach people, one by one, why they had to continue medication once they'd started. They had to deal with the people they found on their porch every morning. They had to drive a full car past desperate people waving their hands weakly in hopes of a ride. They had to keep the car from falling apart. They had to dig it out of the sand or push it out of the mud or find a tractor to haul it out of the river. They had to rush people to the clinic with snake bites. They had to triage children to decide who was most likely to die if they didn't get into the hostel. They stopped everything to pray with people as they withered from the earth.

To avoid operating an ad hoc HIV clinic on their front porch, they set up a slightly more formal clinic in an empty room that belonged to the parish. Medical equipment wasn't much more than a couple of plastic tables and a few chairs. The examination room and waiting room shared the same open space. They had no pharmacy, no medications to dispense. In

Love and Death

hot weather they moved a plastic table out front.

They couldn't resist last requests. They bought meat for an old man who craved that little luxury before he died. They bought coffins for people. When a dying woman requested a Coca-Cola, Diane drove almost 100 km down dirt roads to get her one. Barbara said that wasn't a cost-effective use of gasoline and time. Diane said suppose it was your mother. Barbara then remembered what they were doing in Swaziland. It wasn't just health care and child care. It was compassion. They were there to love—to love and to show love, to show that it's all right to love your neighbor, that love can make life better. The siSwati language didn't even have a word for this kind of love.

Death by death they came to learn that they were dealing with values beyond their understanding. The basic human values they had always assumed innate to all humans were just Judeo-Christian values not necessarily shared by all cultures. They noticed that there were no Down Syndrome children, no children with cleft palates, no congenital deformities whatsoever. But an unusual number of newborns accidentally died while their mothers were washing clothes at the river—drowned, eaten by a crocodile, bitten by a mamba, or meeting some other euphemistic demise. Mothers were capable of infanticide, something the Sisters had simply presumed beyond the instinct of mothers. Even more inexplicably, many people seemed unconcerned with their own survival. The urge to live wasn't present in everyone, and neither was the urge to let-live.

The Sisters couldn't conclude whether this disregard for the most fundamental values was part of the old culture or a new-born product of trauma and poverty. The two overlapped. There was a young woman in their area, for example, whose parents died of AIDS when she was fourteen. That meant she'd been caring for them and the rest of the family for four or five years prior. Her adulthood had begun at about age ten. Soon after her parents died, she was raped and impregnated. She had the baby and at some point contracted HIV. She became pregnant again and endowed her newborn son with the gift of a deadly germ. The Sisters met her when she was 20. She was taking her ARVs and giving them to her child, heading her household reasonably well. In fact, she seemed exceptionally intelligent and capable, so the Sisters hired her to work in the clinic. They taught her to drive. Soon she got a job in a nearby town. But within a few weeks, she started to change. She didn't do her work. She argued with co-workers. She started alienating neighbors who had been trying to help her. She stopped taking her ARVs, and then she stopped giving them to her little boy. And then the little boy fell into a bucket of water and drowned. He was 11 months old.

 As Barbara heard it, the girl had left the baby alone. There was a ten-liter bucket of water in the yard. The boy leaned over the bucket and fell in. But the story didn't ring true. The bucket was higher than the baby. Gravity couldn't pull a baby into it. And there were different stories about how the baby drowned. They didn't add up. As far as Barbara could determine, only

Love and Death

God knew what had happened and understood what the girl had been going through. As Diane saw it, regardless of the details, it was a case like innumerable others—trauma and poverty pushing mothers beyond the realm of motherhood.

The baby's estranged father didn't want his son buried on his homestead. He and the girl weren't married, but since a child always belongs to the father, even if he's a rapist, it should have been buried on his homestead. The chief of the area, who by function of his position was supposed to straighten these situations out, refused to let her bury her child on her own homestead unless she paid the chief a thousand emalangeni, about $125, far more than she could ever come up with. The Sisters made the payment, and the baby was finally put to rest where he belonged.

This cultural confluence of extended clans, sexual exploitation, gender inequality, quasi-feudal government structure, and self-serving morality had been working for many centuries. It might seem cruel, unfair, and inefficient to people raised in the presumptions of Judeo-Christian morality, but it worked to sustain the Swazi society. People reproduced and raised children to adulthood. Extended families took care of orphans and widows. Clans enforced the law. Chiefs and kings took care of politics. Polygamy worked to sustain the population and knit families together. Healers treated life's common illnesses. Society survived. But that cultural system worked only until HIV tossed a bomb into virtually every social institution—family, marriage, tradition, economy, health care, child care, community, education, land rights, and government. Whole families died. The links that held clans together were broken. The moral system enforced by families and clans broke down. The traditional, socially regulated polygamy became an excuse for wanton sex that resulted in disease and babies but not families. Pubescent girls, unprotected by fathers and uncles, faced the inevitability of rape, pregnancy, infection, and infected babies. The loss of a generation of productive workers crippled the economy, and the cost of health programs drained the national treasury. The health system was overwhelmed. Schools were left without teachers, and children faced life with few professional or familial mentors to guide or protect them.

Diane and Barbara were applying love in a place that saw no use in it yet needed it with existential desperation. They didn't try to explain it, didn't push God on anybody, didn't try to draw an overt connection between the behavior-based plague and the tenets of the New Testament. They were simply applying love as best they could and hoping that people would catch on to the possibility that the Christian kind of love could defeat the disease produced by the Swazi kind of love.

Sometimes the application of love involved the pursuit of bad snakes: Cobras that could spit venom ten feet. Pythons longer than that and big enough to swallow a goat. Black mambas. Green mambas. Puff adders half a foot thick. Puff adders account for more deaths in Africa than any other snake, but to Diane they aren't such a problem. They're slow. They stand their ground. Once you know where they are, you have time to kill them. But the mambas are quick and wiggly and a lot more lethal. Like puff adders and pythons, they can be overhead in trees or underfoot along paths. When somebody screams about a snake, everybody comes running. They're so deadly that they cannot be allowed to escape. In their first six months in the country, the Sisters killed a poisonous snake just about every week. One day a black mamba slithered into the house and into Diane's office. Diane did what Jesus would do. She went after it with a knobkierrie and smote the beast. A black mamba bit a thirteen-year-old boy. He died within an hour. The Sisters' 150-pound Rhodesian ridgeback attacked a snake, got bit, and died within ten minutes. Its replacement, two lanky mutts named Boy and Socks, knew how to kill a snake, though they were reluctant to take on the ones that spit. They knew how to prance around a snake, pounce on it, snatch it up, bite it hard, give it a shake, fling it in the air before it could bite, pouncing again and again, two dogs and a pit viper playing cat and mouse. Everybody ran for cover until the flying snake lay still. Then Boy and Socks crouched beside it, bellies to the ground, watching.

Snakes don't wriggle over gravel, so the Sisters' surrounded their house with a band of it. It was disturbing, then, to find a six-foot cobra on the porch in June on the evening of the Feast of the Sacred Heart. Snakes aren't active in June. It was winter. It couldn't have crawled there. Someone had delivered it. The Feast of the Sacred Heart happens to be a special day for Missionary Sisters of the Sacred Heart. The snake did not appear on that date by coincidence. No other snakes appeared inside the gravel zone until one arrived that same year on the evening of December 25. Both snakes were clearly a message even if the message wasn't clear. Was it a warning, an opinion, or a slap to the face of the Christian God, a response to the message of love?

Whatever it was, it didn't work. Nor did it happen again.

Applying love also meant loving a passel of orphans individually. There was no way to love them en masse. Each individual needed individual love. Each had inexpressible emotional baggage. Each needed vigilance and guidance down that rugged path toward becoming a loving human being. The path was especially rugged in Swaziland, of course, and even more so in Lubombo.

During the school year, the children under the Cabrini wing lived in two one-room dormitories, girls in one, boys in the other, about 60 in each, each more than half filled with bunk beds. Each morning at 5:30, everyone got up to take a shower and clean the place. An "auntie" in each dorm oversaw this remarkably disciplined and well organized process. The bunks were moved aside so a crew of assigned children could sweep the floor. They didn't argue with each other; they didn't talk back. They made their beds. They put on blue school uniforms. They shined their raggedy shoes. They combed their close-cropped hair. They ate a breakfast of cornmeal porridge and sour milk (it's supposed to be sour) cooked in big kettles over wood fires. They spooned it up with their fingers and then they

Love and Death

washed their hands at a laundry sink in the yard. Before school they crowded around their auntie to receive pencils that had been broken in half so they'd last until the end of the school year. They ran to school when they heard the bell. They lined up outside, class by class, for twenty minutes of reminders that they were to shine their shoes, comb their hair, and not lose their pencils. They practiced saying the Lord's Prayer, phrase by phrase and class by class until their pronunciation pleased the director. Sometimes they were dispatched to gather firewood from nearby piles, fuel for the cooking of their lunch. When they went, they ran.

During school breaks, each went to a place like home. It might be the homestead of a parent or other relative. It might be the homestead of a gogo—any elderly woman who had a grandmotherly relationship with a child. It might be that of an actual grandmother, but it could be a distant relative or a neighbor or the neighbor of a relative or the relative of a neighbor. Four siblings at the hostel had begun such a journey through homes after their mother died. Three of them were of one father, but the fourth was sure his father was someone else, though he didn't know who. When the father of the three died, the children moved in with a married sister. When her husband died, they all moved in with her in-laws. Her brother-in-law wanted to take the oldest girl as his wife. When she refused, the in-laws kicked all of them off the homestead. They moved from homestead to homestead but were unable to settle anywhere until a gogo took them in. No one knows how the gogo was related to them, whether by blood or friendship or just pity. When someone from St. Philip's went to visit them, the children said they hadn't eaten in two days. Their gogo, they said, had gone to look for a job so she could buy some food. But there are no jobs around St. Philip's, none at all. Food was less likely than starvation, so the four children were taken to the hostel.

Despite their orphanhood and roaming, all the children at the hostel had been at some point attached to a place and a person. The policy, therefore, was that the child needed to belong—to feel a sense of belonging—to a family and community. So that was where they went during school breaks. The Sisters made sure they each took a bag of food staples with them so they weren't a burden on a family. They also checked up on families to make sure no one was being abused or going hungry. Not long after opening the hostel, the Sisters realized that they couldn't take in every child who wanted a better place to live. They had to restrict admittance to the most desperate cases. Some of them were "double orphans" who had lost both parents. Some were "single orphans" whose remaining parent, probably sick and certainly poor, was unable to care for them. Consequently, each child at the hostel was suffering severe emotional trauma and very often such physical trauma as beatings, illness, hunger, and rape. Sexual trauma was not unusual and often undetectable. While most of their parents had died of AIDS, some had suffered something as mundane as being crushed in a car wreck or eaten by a crocodile. These weren't deaths in the distant sterility of a hospital. They happened at home. In the

Love and Death

case of AIDS, they happened over the course of years on the floor of the only room in the house. Those left with one parent in all likelihood suffered hunger and neglect as the remaining parent almost inevitably wasted away of the same disease. Even if relatively healthy, that parent would be struggling to survive in a place of almost zero employment, little water or food, and a lot of extra kids around. UNICEF estimates that there are 100,000 of these children in Swaziland, a painful percentage in a country with a population that barely—and perhaps only temporarily—exceeds one million. The official term for these kids is "Orphaned and Vulnerable Children," a.k.a. OVCs.

Barbara wondered how a nation could raise a generation without any parents. She and Diane and her scant staff were just surrogate parents raising children for surrogate parents. They could provide only minimal care and love for only a thousandth of the OVCs in Swaziland. It was a hard, 24-7-365 job that had to be done carefully, with each individual, over the course of a decade or two. Virtually no one else was doing it. There were no government orphanages. In fact, the government denied the existence of orphans because the culture of the extended family supposedly embraced all children.

Textbooks distributed in Swaziland recognized the problem, but just a bit. They taught children that there were three kinds of families in the country: those with two parents, those with one parent, and those headed by a child. Barbara and Diane found that latter distinction downright offensive. A child cannot head a household. The notion was nothing more than government fantasy.

The Sisters had to raise $3.29 a day to keep a given child fed, healthy, clothed, and loved. The Catholic Church, as a whole, does not fund the Missionary Sisters of the Sacred Heart or any other congregation of women religious. Barbara and Diane had to find funding for everything they did. They pulled every string that connected them to people with money. They immediately spent whatever they raised. Nothing could wait. Children needed food every day. A vehicle without fuel could mean somebody dying. A wheel falling off a vehicle could mean a lot of people dying. When the old Ventura got too undependable for the transport of dying people, they hit up a friend for $25,000 for a new vehicle.

Then they discussed between themselves whether they should be taking the comfy new car with the nice new smell down the rocky, dusty, thorn-bordered trails of the outback to pick up sick people. Barbara suggested it be reserved for more civil trips. Diane asked which car she'd use to take her mother to the hospital. It was a question of efficiency versus humanity. And with no further discussion it was agreed that the nice new car would be used primarily for patients.

Then they got a $100,000 grant for an irrigation system. And then they wondered if it might be enough to produce potable tap water. The whole diocesan mission at St. Philip's—the elementary school, the high school, the hostel and primary care clinic, the hostel and clinic that Barbara and Diane operated, the housing for the staff of these various operations—was using

Love and Death

water pumped directly from the muddy, contaminated Usuthu river. The water was so dirty that pipes clogged with mud. It wasn't something a person would want to drink, though of course for lack of an alternative everyone did. But a modern water system of municipal proportions wasn't something anybody could just go out and buy, not for $100,000 and certainly not in Swaziland.

Then one day a Zimbabwean named Peter Baker, a benefactor of the hostel, cogitated a possibility. He worked at a paint store in Manzini, but he revealed a secret expertise: water systems. He explained how a home-made system could extract filtered water from the river and deliver it to the mission. It was an impossible possibility, but theoretically it could be done. He was willing to offer his expertise. He came out to St. Philip's every weekend to explain each step. He drew pictures for a foreman, Esau. Esau couldn't read but was good at figuring out how to do things, in this case wall off part of the river, dig a vast hole six feet into the riverbed, line its outer perimeter with a filtering wall of stone packed into wire netting, then a wall of pebbles, then a wall of sand. This had to be done in the winter, when the river was low. The only machines were some sad, diesel-fueled pumps that labored day and night to keep some of the water out of the hole. The temperatures were in the 40s (Fahrenheit) and the men had to work wet. They had to find stones and lug them to the site. They had to dig up sand to make cement and mix the cement with shovels. They had to take orders from a nurse and a social worker who were really

253

just figuring out how to build a municipal-sized water system with available materials and not much money. When the Sisters saw the men laboring in the mud and water, they kept giving them raises without being asked. Before it was over, one man died of apparent pneumonia.

They had to build a pump house. They had to learn the mechanics of pumps and the physics of pumping. They had to explain to men how to install the pumps, then teach them to maintain the whole system. They had to learn about chlorine and aluminum. They had to lay pipe up to the mission, build towers for water tanks and then get the tanks up onto the towers. They had to get plumbing installed in buildings. It was a long, hard, impossible project. But once the whole thing got put together, they could open a tap and see clean water come out. They could drink it.

Not bad for a nurse (who at the same time was running a clinic during an epidemic), a social worker (overseeing the care of six score kids, some of them HIV-positive, all of them traumatized) and a bunch of men (some of them HIV-positive, all of them traumatized) who had never dug so much as a well. Such is the power of love.

And so it went. Not much the Sisters took on was anything they'd ever been trained to do, and the difficulties were compounded by Swaziland's lack of infrastructure and its people's lack of training and initiative. There were no construction companies to come in and build something. There were no trucks to deliver pre-mixed cement, no place to buy

Love and Death

concrete blocks. Concrete blocks had to be made, but first molds had to be made, but before that somebody had to come up with lumber and nails and a hammer. Then somebody had to be taught that all the blocks had to be the same size, and then someone had to be taught the right way to build with concrete blocks. When the Sisters hired Esau to build a house for visiting volunteers, he assured them he knew how. And did a pretty good job except that he neglected to make accommodations for plumbing and electricity, two niceties he'd never worked with.

Thus it was with all new staff. They had to begin learning from the most basic level. The only people in Swaziland with any skills beyond primitive agriculture and the weaving of reeds lived in a city. They were not inclined to move to Lubombo for any salary or any reason. The local people had never so much as used a telephone. They couldn't turn on a radio. Few could read or write. They didn't know what time it was or even what time was or even what time was for. Rare was the man who could drive a car.

Work, for people in Lubombo, had always been home-based and slo-mo, moving at the pace of seasons, not minutes. Family life and professional life were one and the same. People naturally assumed Cabrini operated the same way. They stood around talking a lot. They saw no problem with taking time off for a quickie down at the pump house. They brought inter-family squabbles to work. They threatened each other with death and cast spells on each other. The director of personnel, an intelligent, conscientious man invariably in a clean and well pressed button-down shirt, got bewitched so bad he had seizures in the office.

But training local people was part of the mission of child care and health care. To nurture life, the Sisters had to nurture the economy of the region and the professional capacity of its people. The Cabrini Ministries board of directors—all of them Swazis—made a conscious decision to hire local people and to give hiring preference to HIV-positive candidates. They would avoid using foreign volunteers unless they were exceptionally and uniquely qualified. They would pay decent wages. This holistic approach was the only way that their work might extend beyond their stay in Swaziland.

Barbara and Diane were the only people in the country who were working this way—settling in to stay, employing local people, going directly to the ill, working with patients one-on-one, tracking their progress, and dealing with the holistic problem of illness, lack of food, orphaned children, decimated families, unemployment, and a dearth of medication, doctors, water, latrines, transportation, information, employment, technology, compassion, and hope. Benevolent organizations were busy all over southern Africa, but their results were rarely as good as their intentions. They unconsciously assumed they were working with people of culture and values similar to their own. They presumed that people would help each other, volunteer for their own communities, understand what they were told, take a little initiative, take advantage of opportunities in health and education. But these organizations and their people came and went. They rarely if ever stayed long enough to minimally understand the people they were dealing with. Typically, they would contribute the first part—the most visible part—of a long-term project. They might build a school, for example, then leave without finding, training, managing and funding staff. One organization arrived with thousands of tree seedlings. They organized people to plant them. But as soon as the organization left, the same people pulled up all the trees. Someone had told them the trees spread HIV.

It wasn't until the middle of 2011 that Sisters Barbara and Diane, representatives of the Catholic faith, realized they had to negotiate with witch doctors. Despite the presence of a health clinic and perfectly evident results of medication, people still put their faith in sorceresses who rolled bones to diagnose curses. They trusted healers who prescribed bizarre and dangerous remedies. When the medical professionals at the clinic told the Sisters that they, too, respected the healers, the Sisters realized they were still losing the struggle to change attitudes.

The time was ripe. A nurse named Jabulili who had previously worked at Cabrini for 20 years also happened to be a traditional healer, a rather good one with a working knowledge of homeopathy. She offered to help. If Barbara and Diane could get permission from the local chief's "inner council," Jabulili would introduce the Sisters to groups of healers and discuss the possibility of some kind of compromise or mutual effort. Jabulili would lead the discussion.

It had taken seven years to get to the point where a non-Swazi would be trusted enough to discuss this sensitive issue. It wasn't just a matter of health care. It was political. A shift from black magic to medication meant a shift in power. No one likes to give up power, especially not to white foreigners. The last time that had happened, in the 19th century when Swaziland invited the English to protect them from the Dutch, the results had not helped the local people. It was also going to be a radical shift in culture. The Sisters knew that it was not going to happen easily or quickly. After seven years of dispensing medications and compassion, they were just being recognized, just a little bit, as offering something desirable, something good. And it wasn't just the care. It was the caring. It was also the logic, the reason.

"We want to tell the healers, hey, maybe your cures work for some things, but they don't work for HIV and TB," Barbara said as we rumbled down a dirt road toward a clinic in the foothills of the Lubombo mountains. "Our medicine works. You can see the results. But there is a deep spiritual side to Swazis. They believe in a mystical world and have a great desire to maintain that belief. We, on the other hand, are doing the corporal works of mercy—taking care of orphans, the sick, the impoverished."

Those plain, physical good works were bespeaking the value of hope, faith, charity, and good-ol' Christian love. Over the years, the staff at St. Philip's have come to understand this message, and they have changed. Today their communities see them as different. They are seen as people who will help not only on the mission but at home, good people, people who can be trusted not to poison a neighbor or cast a curse. This change, Barbara says, may be one of Cabrini's most significant successes. The connection has been made between the corporal and the spiritual.

*   *   *

By 2012, life was as good as it ever had been. For the first time in seven years, the Sisters were able to slow down a bit. They didn't have a crisis every day. Problems, yes, of course, but problems that could be solved in time. They had seven vehicles on the road. The food supply for the children was pretty steady. Boy and Socks were doing a good job with the snakes. The clinic had just received certification to be a pharmacy. The water system was working as long as there was no power outage, which happened just about every day but rarely all day. Cabrini workers were putting the finishing touches on a comfortable new building for visiting volunteers. Diane said she started crying when she walked into it for the first time since the kitchen was put in, the tile floor laid out, everything looking so civilized. Seven years earlier she'd never imagined such a thing, really had never imagined much more than just getting through another day. And now there she stood, looking through watery eyes at something that seemed a little like a miracle.

Acknowledgments

I would like to thank the Missionary Sisters of the Sacred Heart of Jesus for the opportunity to research and write this book, which has been a dream for many years. I also offer my deepest thanks all the Sisters who, despite their incredibly busy lives, took such good care of me when I visited. They taught me so much about a part of life, and many parts of the world, that I had never known. I offer this book in gratitude.

Special thanks also go to New London Librarium senior editors Ralph Hunter Cheney and Denise Dembinski for their sharp and unforgiving editorial comments. Thanks are also due artist Colleen Hennessy for allowing the use of her painting on the cover of this book. And the author thanks his wife, Solange Aurora Cavalcante Cheney for giving him the time and freedom necessary to produce this book.

About Sister Barbara Staley

Sr. Barbara Staley has been a Missionary Sister of the Sacred Heart of Jesus since 1988. She has a bachelor's degree in Education from Clarion University of Pennsylvania and a Masters of Social Work from New York University. She has worked with many poor and marginalized populations within the United States and abroad. Her work has included working with the developmentally disabled in residential care settings, providing counseling to street children in New York City, helping undocumented immigrants with accessing health care and social services in Chicago, providing mental health services to the mentally ill and to persons with addictions, activities of human promotion in Guatemala, and establishing a clinic in the outback of Swaziland to help persons with HIV, their families, and orphans.

In 2013 Sister Barbara was named General Superior of her religious congregation. The organization of women religious, which has borne the missionary legacy of St. Frances Xavier Cabrini since 1880, is active in 15 countries on six continents. For more information, see mothercabrini.org and msccabrini.org.

About Glenn Alan Cheney

Glenn Alan Cheney is the author of more than 25 fiction and nonfiction books, hundreds of articles, and several essays and poems. He has also translated books from Portuguese to English. His books cover a wide variety of topics, including Brazil's Quilombo dos Palmares and Estrada Real, Chernobyl, Abraham Lincoln, Pope Francis, the Pilgrims, bees, Swaziland, human and environmental issues in Amazonia, nuclear proliferation, and Central American politics. He is managing editor of New London Librarium. He resides in Hanover, Conn., with his wife, Solange.

www.ingramcontent.com/pod-product-compliance
Lightning Source LLC
Chambersburg PA
CBHW030332230426
43661CB00032B/1381/J